The Theory and Practice of Security Analysis

MICHAEL A. NICOLAOU

MACMILLAN
Business

First published 2000 by
MACMILLAN PRESS LTD
Houndmills, Basingstoke, Hampshire RG21 6XS
and London
Companies and representatives
throughout the world

ISBN 0–333–72712–6 hardcover ✓
ISBN 0–333–72713–4 paperback

A catalogue record for this book is available
from the British Library.

This book is printed on paper suitable for recycling and
made from fully managed and sustained forest sources.

10   9   8   7   6   5   4   3   2   1
09 08 07 06 05 04 03 02 01 00

Copy-edited and typeset by Povey–Edmondson
Tavistock and Rochdale, England

Printed and bound in Great Britain by
Antony Rowe Ltd, Chippenham, Wiltshire

THE THEORY AND PRACTICE OF
SECURITY ANALYSIS

Contents

List of Figures

List of Tables

Preface

While this book touches on some of the many mainstream models of security analysis (this forms the theoretical aspect), it also refers to the empirical findings or summarised insights of various writers (this usually forming the practical aspect). Although it purposely aims to be eclectic rather than draw from the experiences of the author, it is hoped that the approach of combining theory with practice is particularly useful to the early City entrant who is currently doing the rounds before finally specialising. Many of the examples are drawn from writers in the USA, but this should not detract from the general insights they offer. As a summarised introduction, the theory is a prerequisite to the context in which the discussion should be placed. In some cases, however, I have gone beyond this, and although much of the practical implications for security analysis and investment management had their genesis in the field of academic research, this book is not aimed at discussing esoteric aspects of academic relevancy.

The focus is purposely on the more traditional analyses since, although many theories have evolved into powerful new ones, their starting point is still fundamentally traditional. The need to decompose complex financial arrangements into their constituent elements is as important today as it has ever been, and the basic premise underlying plain vanilla options has been expanded to include exotic options. Although an alternative theory now exists, the equilibrium-pricing model known as the Capital Asset Pricing Model (CAPM) still forms a framework for analysis and is used by practitioners as an analogue to communicate both simple and complex market events. The link between equities and bonds has been hypothesised under a number of theories. This book is therefore somewhat unusual in introducing the traditional types of each of the main asset classes: bonds (gilt-edged stock) and equities. This is supported by a brief introduction to the theory of bond and equity relationships, extracts on the strategic value of real options and an introduction to equity warrants and equity convertibles.

While in practice investment decisions require analysis and judgement within a dynamic framework, in this book we facilitate the exposition by making simplified assumptions, by discussing models (an alternative name for theories) that help to provide a less ambiguous analysis. But in writing a book on security analysis, one is cognisant that many readers will be interested to know what class of security and which within that class should be bought or sold to make a profit. Clearly, the panacea of profitable security analysis is in analysing and drawing correct conclusions about the markets' motive force to ownership of securities at every instant in time. This, however, is not our purpose since such an answer cannot be given without knowledge of the relationship between securities and markets prevailing at the time such a decision is made and based on the circumstances, knowledge and detailed analysis of all the material factors of the minute. This forces the reader to research securities in a dynamic environment. Nevertheless, it is hoped that this book forms a worthwhile addition in helping to understand that research.

Putting together this book meant I was left to the mercy of a computer. Therefore, I would like to thank Carol R. M. Barnes whose computer expertise was so valuable and whose proximate support tempered my inclination to give up at times when my computer found another reason to fail.

I would also like to express my gratitude to J. Reid and Francis Kelly and my sincere thanks to everyone involved in the book at my publishers and Povey–Edmondson, in particular the main individuals with whom I had the pleasure of dealing, namely Stephen Rutt and Keith Povey.

Michael A. Nicolaou

The author and publishers are grateful to the following for permission to reproduce copyright material: The Free Press, a division of Simon & Schuster, for Figures 4.3 and 4.4 from *Competitive Strategy: Techniques for Analyzing Industries and Competitors* by Michael E. Porter, © 1980 by the Free Press, © 1980 by Michael E. Porter; Primark Datastream for Figures 3.3, 5.1. 5.3 and 6.3, © Primark Datastream; McKinsey & Co for the use of a number of works in Chapters 4, 5 and 7, © by McKinsey & Co.; Goldman Sachs International Ltd relating to the work 'Do Global Stock Prices Need to Fall by 40%?', © 1992 by Goldman Sachs; and the Bank of England, particularly in relation to the article 'Equity Prices and Financial Stability', © 1998 by the Bank of England. Every effort has been made to contact all the copyright-holders, but if any have been inadvertently omitted the publishers will be pleased to make the necessary arrangement at the earliest opportunity.

List of Abbreviations

APT	arbitrage pricing theory
bp(s)	basis point(s)
CAPM	Capital Asset Pricing Model
CD	Certificate of Deposit
CML	Capital Market Line
DCF	discounted cash flow
DDB	deep discount bond
DPVI	difference in present value of income
EMH	efficient market hypothesis
EPS	earnings per share
FFC	fixed finance costs
FOC	fixed operating costs
IGM	interest gearing multiplier
IL	index-linked
LSV	level of sales volume
MPC	marginal propensity to consume
MPT	modern portfolio theory
NPV	net present value
OP	operating profit
OPEC	Organisation of Petroleum-Exporting Countries
OPM	operational price multiplier
OVM	operational volume multiplier
P&L	profit and loss
PBT	profit before tax
P/DIV	price to dividend
P/E	price to earnings
p/s	price to sales
PVBP	price value of a basis point
ROCE	return on capital employed
RPI	Retail Price Index
RPIX	Retail Price Index excluding mortgage financing
S/MC	sales-to-equity market capitalisation
SML	security market line
SORP	Statement of recommended practice
SPU	sales price per unit
SSAP	Statement of Standard Accounting Practice
TM	total multiplier
VCU	variable costs per unit
+	rising (graph axes)
−	falling (graph axes)

Part I

Background and Financial Market Theory

1 Introduction

Economic markets have changed significantly over the past twenty-five years or so. International trade, partly driven by the notion of comparative advantage, has expanded on a global scale, as the world's population has demanded an ever-increasing variety of goods and services from higher standards of living. This has also meant that countries have become increasingly interdependent, so that many political and economic events thousands of miles away might now have economic implications back home.

In an attempt to discipline economic and financial markets and foster international trade and investment, periods have been experienced with fixed exchange rates between certain member countries. However, economic and monetary policy harmonisation was usually unpalatable for some member nations with the result that the established parities became strained. For example, the break-up of the so-called 'snake' and the subsequent sharp oil price hikes of the 1970s temporarily increased the volatility associated with financial markets and the risks associated with investment in goods and services. It also expanded the notion of volatility from purely short-term domestic considerations to include international factors. Considerations such as these encouraged borrowers and lenders to seek improved ways to align their assets and liabilities.

To better meet their needs, borrowers increasingly looked to the capital markets where innovative solutions to their requirements could be more easily structured. As a result, much of the corporate funding traditionally sourced from commercial banks began to diminish (a trend known as bank *disintermediation*). This helped accelerate the growth in swaps, futures, options and other instruments that could be used to better match the needs of borrowers and lenders alike. It is now possible to hedge currency risk, interest rate risk and commodity price risk far more satisfactorily. These developments were underwritten by the parallel support shown by investors in capital markets and promoted by the introduction of complex financial engineering techniques.

Money

Money is known to all of us. We use it to buy our daily food, pay for our gas, electricity, holidays and possibly to have a flutter on the horses. In this way, money is used as a *medium of exchange*. To facilitate this, money is also used

3

as a *unit of account*, enabling all things that are traded or exchanged to be measured, thus overcoming many of the problems associated with the old barter system. In the context of financial securities, money is used as a medium by a market participant to buy some kind of paper – for example, a bond certificate or a share certificate – that indicates title to certain relevant future rights. To the issuer of money debt, it is a medium by which it incurs the liability and later settles it (capital and interest). In this way, money is also used as a *medium for deferred payments*.

As a medium for deferred payments, money is also used as a *store of value*. Its use as a store of value arises from savings where income is not spent on current consumption. In a modern society, low-risk, easy-access deposit accounts help in the management of future short-term expenditure patterns. However, much of the amount saved is also likely to find its way into the money and capital markets as a relatively longer-term form of saving. These forms of saving are often channelled through banks, building societies, life, pensions and general insurance organisations and unit trust companies, as well as friendly societies and investment trusts (closed-end funds). The huge amount of savings these institutions are entrusted to manage means the interaction of their collective buying and selling can be an important influential factor on the prices found in financial markets.

Money markets

The money markets form a closely related but perceptibly distinguishable part of financial markets. While activity in the money markets also encompasses non-negotiable debt, such as inter-bank deposits, 'repos' and 'reverses', the range of instruments that are negotiable includes Treasury bills, bills of exchange, certificates of deposit, commercial paper, euronotes (issued under a variety of funding structures) and euro-commercial paper.

Treasury bills have historically formed part of the government's financing operations. With unmatched income and expenditure patterns, the issuance of Treasury bills helps meet a resulting short-term financing gap. Commercial bills of exchange are typically used to help finance trade. They may be drawn on the issuer (a trade bill) or on a bank (a bank bill or a banker's acceptance). Euronotes are syndicated arrangements that offer short-term finance during a much longer rolling time horizon.

Two of the main money-market instruments are commercial paper and certificates of deposit. Commercial paper is issued by companies and is usually unsecured. Unlike commercial bills, the money raised is used for many purposes, for example, this type of financing might be used to manage working capital needs. Although some commercial paper issuance is in interest form, the more common covenants the face value (also known as the par value, principal value or nominal value). Some money-market instruments are generally issued in interest form, including a certificate of deposit issued by a bank or building society in recognition of a deposit. The Bank of England has also allowed discount issues and floating rate certificates of deposit as well as features such as puts or calls.

It is often possible to make mathematical comparisons between many money-market instruments and other products that generate a logical pattern of future cash flows. These include fixed-coupon medium-term notes in their final coupon period, and, effectively, between many fixed-income bonds in their final coupon pay-period. By making further assumptions, cases where these are in their final year with more than one coupon outstanding can also be accommodated to help make more meaningful comparisons. In the US market, for example, it is common to convert Treasury Bill discount rates to quote some *equivalent bond yield* (or *coupon yield equivalent*) to facilitate comparison with the convention employed with US Treasury Notes and Bonds. This may still be done, notwithstanding the fact that one may also need to take account of other practical differences, such as the liquidity in each market.

The non-limiting use of funds raised by many money markets instruments means they can be combined in ways to optimise the servicing cost of funding. Alternatively, they may offer arbitrage income to the arranger or holder. For example, they can be integrated with forward foreign exchange. If the extra return outweighs the extra cost of hedging the eventual *transaction risk* (the realised effect of mismatched currency moves), arbitrage opportunities arise. However, overseas investing creates other potential risks and rewards, such as political risk and potentially differing tax implications.

Financial valuation theory

In economics, price is distinguished from value. In general, value represents what a good is considered to be worth while price is the amount of money for which it can be exchanged. The concept of value is often used in a generalised sense and measured in a variety of ways. Investment value is often described as the capitalised value of a future cash flow stream when discounted back at an appropriate rate of interest (see Williams, 1938).

Most types of securities involve two types of cash flow: an initial cash outflow and a subsequent series of cash inflows. Fixed income government bonds offer a series of covenanted cash flows whereas the cash flows associated with equities needs to be forecast. Rather than have a varying rate of interest, a single, constant rate of interest is sometimes assumed to discount the cash flows to the present time. This rate of interest forms a special case in a much larger universe of possible interest rates.

Although we ignore tax in this book (unless stated otherwise), associated with the notion of investment value is a net-of-tax measure that takes tax into account. A further measure involves calculating a 'real' (inflation adjusted) rate of interest that takes into account the impact of some measure of inflation. There is one class of security where inflation is explicit to understanding the investment characteristics of that security, and this is in reference to index-linked gilt-edged stock (see Chapter 3).

Perspectives of risk

In practice, risk and uncertainty are related issues. Therefore, the two terms are often used analogously because both would normally involve objective and subjective considerations. However, in economics there is a distinction between risk that can be quantified and uncertainty that cannot be quantified (a distinction we generally avoid for the sake of simplicity in this book).

Some investors are concerned with risk effects in their downside form (the potential for loss or benchmark underperformance). However, many quantitative measures of risk tend to be more balanced because a market includes both buyers and sellers and because it helps to open the mind to a consideration of all possible outcomes and thus helps to highlight the consequences of alternative decisions.

For example, consider a hypothetical investor holding a diversified equity portfolio whose performance is measured relative to some benchmark. This investor considers only downside risk and has concluded that the equity market, where the fund has exposure, will fall. Suppose the decision is taken to withdraw all the invested funds from the market. These funds are then placed on interest-bearing deposit with a bank, say. The risk is not that this decision is right, but that it is wrong. The fund is then exposed to the risk that the equity market and the equities it would have held rise significantly enough to make the returns from holding cash look derisory. Economists would describe such a perspective of risk as the *opportunity cost* (meaning the sacrificed alternative) of not being invested.

Other perspectives of risk are also important. For example, many borrowers have liabilities to meet so aim to match the servicing costs of those liabilities with assets in ways that reduce this risk. In this sense, risk is not associated with a relative or absolute return, but with a market position for the assets that does not match the servicing requirements of the underlying liabilities. For example, some financial institutions write over-the-counter derivatives which, in order to hedge their potential liabilities, might establish counter positions using other derivatives.

Demand and supply theory

An economist's view of a perfect market (with perfect competition between the participants) consists of many buyers and sellers with no single entity able to affect the market price of a good and with equal information flow across the market. The world's major financial markets can be seen to be situations in which there are many buyers and sellers of securities, with investors well-informed given the revolution in communication technology and the now large multinational information service providers. At one time, there were onerous conditions attached to stock market membership, and market making for specified groups of shares was often concentrated in a small number of jobbers. Since the 1980s 'Big Bang', the activity within the London Stock Exchange more properly conforms to economists' theoretical concept of a perfect market. (The equity capital of many smaller companies is usually traded in an environment more akin to some form of imperfect market.)

The demand for a good is the quantity for which there are willing and able buyers (effective demand) in the market at a given price over some time interval. The supply of a good is the quantity for which there are willing and able suppliers (effective supply) in the market at a given price over some time interval (as a simplification, we assume all demand is effective in this book). Although economic theory recognises there can be exceptions, a common assumption is that under *ceteris paribus* (which we shall take to mean *all other things being constant*) the quantity demanded is negatively related to a change in market price over some time interval. Under the same assumption, the quantity supplied is positively related to a change in market price over some time interval. The (unique) price that causes the combined effect of these forces to be equal is called the equilibrium price (in the sense of demand and supply).

As we have assumed that all factors other than price are held constant (under the *ceteris paribus* condition), this theory of demand and supply is essentially a short-term phenomenon (sometimes, this short period can last for only a few seconds in financial markets). In practice the demand and supply of a good over a longer period of time is determined by more than just price. Economic theory then distinguishes between price changing the quantity demanded and the quantity supplied (under *ceteris paribus*) from a change in demand and a change in supply at all prices (arising from factors other than price). If security prices take a random walk around the *ceteris paribus* equilibrium price, this broader demand and supply concept allied to the random arrival of new information helps to elicit one of the older requirements under the efficient market hypothesis (see later).

One of the additional conditions required for perfect competition is that the goods under consideration be homogeneous. However, not all bonds and equities are homogeneous. One bond may offer dissimilar returns and have a different risk profile from another in terms of coupon, term to maturity, credit quality and features such as an embedded option. In the case of equities, different companies have varying risk profiles and profitable opportunities. There will therefore be many prices where the prospective risk and return profiles of owning securities are not homogeneous.

Although the notion of heterogeneity is a valid reflection of securities markets, an investigation of asset classes typically entails a relaxation of this pragmatic aspect. Thus, particular types of financial securities can be grouped together as a homogeneous class even if the individual constituents of that class are not strictly homogeneous. Thus, UK equities in general or fixed-income government guaranteed bonds in general may be viewed as being separate groups. When this is the case, the additional generalised assumption is often made that it is possible to represent, by some type of indicator, features of that asset class such as its price and yield. This might be given by an appropriate equity market index or perhaps a particularly good liquid bond issue that is broadly accepted by the market as a standard and thus being representative of fixed-income government bond yields in general. Then, if the indicator rises, in general the individual constituents of that asset class have also risen; if the indicator falls, in general the individual constituents of that asset class have also fallen. Under such assumptions, certain models have been cast that conceptualise relationships between equities and fixed-income government bonds as asset classes (see Chapter 6).

Price convergence and arbitrage

Although there is a natural tendency for homogeneous securities in a visibly priced market to converge, the theory of arbitrage pricing is also used in a more general way in the financial markets to price synthesised financial products. For example, a financially engineered futures contract (synthetic futures) may be created to be similar to an equity index futures contract. Depending upon the borrowing rate and assumptions about the relative cash flows, this relationship can be mathematically measured. Since the synthetic futures would attempt to replicate the pay-off from the futures contract, dissimilar standardised prices might offer arbitrage opportunities.

Arbitrage trading opportunities occur where the future benefits of owning securities are similar or homogeneous, but are in some way thought to be mispriced with respect to each other. This mispricing might occur during times of market upheavals or in other situations. The arbitrageur would sell the relatively expensive securities and simultaneously buy the alternative, similar or homogeneous, securities where they were being offered more cheaply.

Where an exposure can be offset exactly, arbitrage is often described as being risk-free. For example, imagine an arbitrageur considering a particular security: this security is sold at a higher price and a simultaneous route found to buy it at a lower price. The difference is often said to be a risk-free profit. *Ceteris paribus*, the effect is that the higher price in the market will tend to fall and the lower price will tend to rise. In theory, risk-free arbitrage will continue until the two prices become equal. The security is then said to be in equilibrium (in the sense of arbitrage-free possibilities).

In practice, arbitrage will occur where the extra benefits are not outweighed by other considerations, such as the additional transaction expenses in creating (and potentially closing) an arbitrage position and the risks associated with an adverse move in price between concomitant trades. Nevertheless, where risk-free arbitrage is efficacious across a market, arbitrage opportunities will quickly dissipate and the prices of homogeneous securities would converge.

Efficient market hypothesis

The notion of market efficiency has had a long history. It deals with a number of aspects of market pricing, but is essentially concerned with classes of information and the quality of the market pricing mechanism to impound that information (for a development of the theory, see Peters, 1996, Ch. 2). Given the quality of the information services available to market operators and advances in communication technology, active fund management is now, to some extent, about management of the value generation process from the flow of information. Index funds implicitly assume the purest form of market efficiency, although contrary to what was one of the many interpretations of the theory, one premise does not require that the true economic or intrinsic value be equal to the market price over all continuous time points. The true active fund manager takes an antithetical view and applies a dynamic approach to managing a portfolio.

The empirical evidence on the efficient market hypothesis (EMH) is large and varied (this is reviewed in a number of works, such as Fama, 1991, and Lofthouse, 1994, Ch. 18). In testing the various levels of the EMH, the approach sometimes taken has involved a model of price behaviour implying that two simultaneous aspects were being tested: the validity of pricing model used and the EMH. As a result, the theory itself could not actually be tested (this point is recognised in Fama, 1991). On a more pragmatic level, many of the scheduled and proposed changes to the sterling government bond market by HM Treasury in 1995 were anticipated in market pricing and this forms one manifestation of bond market efficiency (see Bank of England, 1995). Some security markets have been described as 'inefficient' (for example, the equity convertible market: see McGuire, 1990). Regulators to many of the major securities markets have attempted to ensure a more equitable market environment by establishing a regulatory framework on insider trading abuse.

Some accepted the theory which claimed that the efficient (in terms of expected return and standard deviation as a measure of portfolio risk) market exposure is simply the market portfolio. However, since it was not possible to reproduce this theoretical market portfolio, an alternative concerned itself with replicating a sub-set of the market portfolio such as an index. Equity fund managers that hold replicated index portfolios are now said to manage (equity) index funds. The practical difficulties associated with reproducing an index exactly means that some funds now simply track an equity index and these fund managers are said to manage (equity) tracker funds. A variant tracker type fund is structured with the objective of minimising index tracking error but where the fund manager simultaneously has a bias in the fund to emphasise certain desired characteristics.

Portfolio theory

Portfolio theory deals with how portfolio choice can be enacted. Asset pricing theories attempt to assess the motive force to security ownership and how security equilibrium pricing might be established. Efficient markets theory (under historical interpretations) deals with the efficiency with which the existing information universe (or new information) is priced into security pricing. The combination of these influences on general investment thinking is very broadly known as modern portfolio theory (MPT).

Under MPT, market participants need to be rewarded for their risk exposure. They will accept the lowest risk way of achieving any given expected return and are said to be risk-averse. Markowitz (1959) quantified a measure of portfolio risk as the statistical measure of standard deviation (or variance). Standard deviation has a number of favourable attributes since it considers all possible outcomes and it is possible to form a sub-set to consider only particular aspects of the distribution of outcomes. Statistically, however, it can be an ambiguous indicator of the degree of concentration of a distribution about the average outcome because of antithetical considerations (see, for example, Peters, 1996, Chs 3, 6 and 7). Nevertheless, its use has allowed the development of a theory that is part of the colloquial vocabulary of the analyst and fund manager.

To help explain how expected return and risk might be linked, asset-pricing theories evolved. Probably the most well known equilibrium asset pricing theory is the Capital Asset Pricing Model (CAPM). MPT asserts that total risk comprises both the risk affecting a security (*unsystematic* or *specific risk*) and the risk generally influencing all securities (*systematic* or *market risk*). In

Figure 1.1 *An example of diversification*

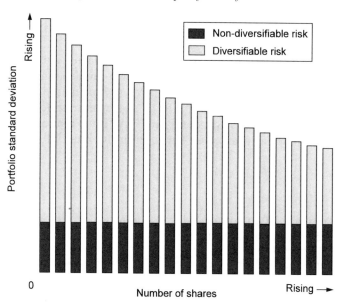

the context of MPT, because standard deviation as a measure of total risk divides into that which is diversifiable (unsystematic risk) and that which is not diversifiable (systematic risk), a market that is priced in such a way that it eliminates diversifiable risk will only reward non-diversifiable risk. As an example, this is illustrated in Figure 1.1. If markets are priced in a way which rewards only systematic risk, then it will not be optimal (in terms of expected return and standard deviation as a measure of portfolio risk) to hold a portfolio that is not diversified. A collection of securities that is optimal in terms of the trade-off between standard deviation (as a measure of portfolio risk) and expected return is termed an *efficient portfolio*. The CAPM then derives theoretical implications for individual securities (see Chapter 5).

It should be remembered that for any individual security, the cause of risk and return may be related to any number of reasons, but the measures of these effects under the CAPM approach is, respectively, systematic risk and a related measure known as beta. Subjective considerations beyond these remain the domain of the active fund manager, but the CAPM approach only applies assumptions that are homogeneous for all investors.

The simple version of the CAPM was based on the intuitive premise that all securities are exposed to a beta effect. There are, however, a number of security attributes and the model has been tested against additional sensitivities (see the reviews in Lofthouse, 1994). More recent research has focused on the formulation of multi-factor models. The arbitrage pricing theory (APT), initially developed by Ross (1976), provides an alternative basis for the relationship between factor risks and returns. APT asserts that prices should impound systematic factors' to reflect arbitrage-free positions. APT does not pre-specify the systematic factors.

Empirically, APT factors include financial and macro-economic variables (see Chen, Roll and Ross, 1986). The practical implications of APT risk factors means that a forecast of unanticipated (by the market) factor values can be formulated into an active APT management strategy (see Berry, Burmeister and McElroy, 1998). Alternatively, APT might be used in a passive equity fund management sense (see Berry, Burmeister and McElroy, 1988).

Cost of money

Interest rates are often influenced by a number of factors, which may arguably include, in no particular order of importance:

- the demand for credit by the government, commercial organisations and individuals;
- the level of liquidity in the savings market as determined by both domestic and cross-border flows of savings;
- the relative value of competing investments.

Apart from official interest rates, there are many other interest rates in financial markets that can relate to that current in the secondary markets for existing debt securities according to the term to maturity, coupon, credit quality of the issue or issuer, level of liquidity and so on. The importance of official interest rates to influence market determined rates of interest clearly has implications for UK monetary policy (see, for example, Dale, 1993).

In an MPT world, a risky asset is expected to generate a return above the riskless rate of interest. However, a hedger is exposed to risk and wants to defray part or all of that risk exposure. Therefore, consider the creation of a call option, C, whose value at time $t = 0$ is $C_{t=0}$. This pays out only at some future point in time $t = T$ a sum contingent on the value of a non-income-generating ordinary share, S, whose current price in the market is $S_{t=0}$. The pay-off from $C_{t=0}$ at time $t = T$ is $S_{t=T}$ for a fixed price of K if $S_{t=T} > K$ or zero otherwise. Thus:

$$C_{t=T} = \begin{cases} S_T - K \text{ if } S_T > K \\ \text{or} \\ 0 \text{ otherwise} \end{cases}$$

While there are many different hedging strategies, consider the situation where at time $t = 0$ a quantity of $S_{t=0}$ is held such that its value varies inversely to the contingent claim arising from the sold position in $C_{t=0}$. At the next forward instant in time, $t = \delta_t$ (not beyond time T), the value of the position will reflect the values of $S_{\delta t}$ and $C_{\delta t}$. However, to be an exact hedge requires that the position at $t = 0$ less the present value of the position dictated at time $t = \delta_t$ be equal to zero.

If such a hedge could be unambiguously quantifiable, then it could be said to be riskless. In theory, a riskless arrangement should not demand a risk premium above the riskless rate in market equilibrium. Further, in a riskless arbitrage-free market, returns are not supposed to be free. A perfect hedge would thus not pay out more or less than is necessary to cover the pay-off from the contingent liability at maturity. Although there are other possible hedging strategies, the situation under investigation might involve an initial quantity of S set against a riskless asset (yielding the riskless rate of interest). But there are an infinite number of time instants between time $t = 0$ and time $t = T$ and such a hedge will require adjustment (so-called rebalancing). This means continuously and instantaneously adjusting the proportions of S held against the riskless asset over time to maintain the hedge. To help make the hedge theoretically perfect means the amount from adjusting the quantity of S must exactly offset the amount from adjusting the quantity of the risk-free asset. A perfect hedge would also align its behaviour in exactly the same way as C does throughout the period of the hedge. If a set of assumptions were quantified that allowed the above theoretical arguments to work, then it would be possible to quantify the theoretical value of $C_{t=0}$.

One probability based option valuation theory is that given by Black and Scholes (1973). The formula (see Chapter 7) does not incorporate a parameter for the expected growth rate in the underlying. If such a hypothetical world existed, known as a *risk-neutral world*, investors can be viewed as having an expectation for the rate of return that equates to the riskless rate of interest. Although investors do incorporate their risk preferences when valuing the underlying in the real world, this argument nevertheless lends itself to a simpler approach to the option valuation theory known as the *risk-neutral valuation method* first introduced by Cox and Ross (1976). (Because the basis can be viewed as a theoretical hedging strategy that is riskless, it is intuitively possible to reconcile the notion of option value in a risk-neutral world with that in a world in which all investors are risk-averse so long as the share price is the same in both worlds. A less obvious rationale is discussed in Galitz, 1994, Ch. 10.)

Layout of the book

This book is divided into four further parts. Part II introduces the main UK fixed-income government bond types. Part III introduces a number of internal and external corporate operating considerations and the theory of equity security analysis. Part IV introduces the concept of portfolio construction and asset class relationships. Part V is concerned with real options and certain equity option related securities.

Although we round quantities in this book, this rounding and the number of decimal places taken is totally arbitrary and does not follow any market convention. Unless stated otherwise, we assume all interest rates are positive and there are no transaction expenses and no taxation. Finally, by its very nature, much of the exposition involves knowledge of the mathematics of finance. Although we attempt to keep this to a minimum, this should not be a hurdle to the readership this book is aimed at.

References and further reading

Bank of England (1995) *Gilts and the Gilt Market, Review 1994–1995* (March) (London: Bank of England).

Black, F. and M. Scholes (1973) 'The Pricing of Options and Corporate Liabilities', *Journal of Political Economy*, vol. 81, no. 3 (May/June), pp. 637–54.

Berry, M. A., E. Burmeister, and M. B. McElroy (1988) 'Sorting Out Risks Using Known APT Factors', *Financial Analysts Journal*, March–April, pp. 29–42.

Chen, N., Roll, R. and Ross, S. A. (1986) 'Economic Forces and the Stock Market', *Journal of Business*, vol. 59, no. 3, pp. 383–403.

Cox, J. and S. Ross (1976) 'The Valuation of Option for Alternative Stochastic Processes', *Journal of Financial Economics*, vol. 3 (January), pp. 145–66.

Dale, S. (1993) *The Effect of Official Interest Rate Changes on Market Rates since 1987*, Bank of England Working Paper Series No. 10 (April) (London: Bank of England).

Fama, E. F. (1991) 'Efficient Capital Markets: II', *Journal of Finance*, vol. XLVI, no. 5 (December), pp. 1575–611.

Galitz, L. (1994), *Financial Engineering – Tools and Techniques to Manage Financial Risk* (London: Pitman Publishing).

Lofthouse, S. (1994) *Equity Investment: How to Select Stocks and Markets* (Chichester: John Wiley).

Markowitz, H. M. (1959) *Portfolio Selection: Efficient Diversification of Investments* (New York: John Wiley).

McGuire, S. R. (1990) *The Handbook of Convertibles* (Cambridge: Woodhead-Faulkner).

Peters, E. E. (1996) *Chaos and Order in the Capital Markets* (New York: John Wiley).

Ross, S. (1976) 'The Arbitrage Theory of Capital Asset Pricing', *Journal of Economic Theory*, vol. 13 (December), pp. 341–60.

Williams, J. B. (1938) *The Theory of Investment Value* (Cambridge, Mass.: Harvard University Press).

Part II

Bond Securities

2 Fixed-Income Gilt-Edged Stock and Related Variations

The gilt-edged market

In practice, a distinction is made between corporate issued bonds and those of a government. For example, other than Treasury bills, *gilt-edged stocks* (or simply 'gilts') is a generic term usually used to describe bonds issued by the government of the UK. It has been traditional for most gilts to pay coupons net of tax, although these can now be paid before deduction of withholding tax, a situation available since 6 April 1998 for registered bondholders.

The gilt market encompasses a range of issues with particular features. They are usually classed as either floating rate, index-linked or conventional (this last representing any that are not classed as floating rate or index-linked). As part of the Bank of England's relationship with the gilt-edged market makers (responsibility for the management of the gilt market having since been transferred to the UK Debt Management Office), the Bank has historically undertaken few transactions that changed the nature of the outstanding stock.

The market value of outstanding gilts as at 31 March 1998 is shown in Figure 2.1. The market value proportion of floating rate and undated issues has remained fairly stable over the period 1995 to 1998, while that for index-linked gilts has grown and that for conventional stock has fallen. This reflects not only the changing relative demand and supply conditions in the markets, but the issuance needs of the authorities and the relative amount of each type

Figure 2.1   *Outstanding value proportions of gilts as at 31 March 1998*

Market value proportions of outstanding gilts

Floating rate (2.7%)	Index-linked (17.9%)	Undated (0.5%)	Other conventional (78.9)

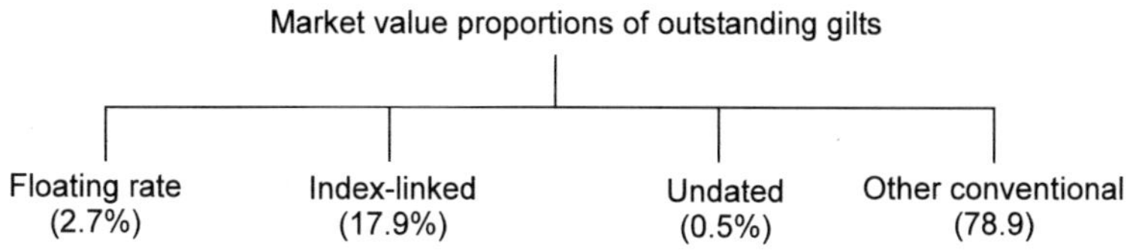

Source: Bank of England.

of stock maturing. In the case of index-linked, it also reflects the inflation indexation on the outstanding bonds.

Gilts have been brought to market in a number of ways although, over more recent years, the authorities have favoured an auction process for conventional gilts with the number of primary issues using this method having steadily increased since 1992. Tap issues (sold to market makers) are now more commonly used as part of the discretionary management policy of the authorities rather than as part of an initiative for the issuance of new gilts (other than for index-linked gilts historically, although even here the policy aim of moving towards an auction process has more recently been instigated).

General bond classifications and risk considerations

There is a range of generalised bond classifications including the following.

1   *Bearer bonds* These are also called unregistered bonds (in contrast to that of registered bonds) since the owner is not registered in the books of the issuer (or the issuer's registrar). With bearer fixed-income bonds, the periodic interest amount will be paid at the appropriate time via the presentation of a coupon attached to the bond certificate. Whether a fixed-income bond is bearer or not, each of these periodic interest amounts is now commonly referred to as a coupon (and when expressed as a percentage of the par value is known as a *coupon rate*).

2   *Foreign bonds* These are usually issued in the domestic currency of the country of issue by a foreign borrower. For example, these have been dubbed 'bulldog bonds' when sold in the UK, 'yankee bonds' when sold in the USA and 'samurai bonds' when sold in Japan.

3   *Eurobonds* These generally represent any bond denominated in a euro-currency and issued in the eurobond markets. London is a major eurobond trading centre (with the London Stock Exchange having listed an increased number of eurobonds over more recent years).

The risk characteristics of fixed-income bonds generally include the following.

1   *Default risk (sometimes called credit risk)* This is associated with the obligation to pay the covenanted cash flows on a bond so will include insolvency or even a credit downgrade. Some corporate bond issues are made by associates or subsidiaries of large international groups of companies for which the parent might act as guarantor to the issue.

    For many of the larger bond issuers, there exist professional credit rating agencies that can give an informed opinion on the relative interest-

and capital-paying capacity and willingness of the issuer, and on the asset backing to an issue. A credit rating analysis associated with a particular bond issue would, inevitably, involve both qualitative and quantitative factors important to the bond issue, its issuer and its lenders. There are many considerations, but for a corporate issue these would usually include an assessment of its industry characteristics and its competitive positioning therein. More generally, financial risk considerations include the degree and method of financing and the issuer's ability to service current and known future external financing needs as well as the nature of a bond issue such as its priority in repayment compared to any current and known future obligations.

2   *Interest rate risk* This is associated with a change in the price of a fixed-income bond resulting from a change in interest rates. The measure of interest rate used is usually related to a bond's yield.

3   *Inflation risk* This is associated with the diminishing 'real' (inflation-adjusted) purchasing power of a given amount of money. As a result, it is often thought to have a powerful impact on yields found on fixed-income bonds. Fisher's (1965) theory is discussed in Brealey and Myers (1996, Ch. 23) where it is argued that it is money (non-inflation adjusted) bond yields in the market that adjust to changes in expected inflation, so the real yield should be somewhat stable under this theory. Empirical results by Barr and Pesaran (1995) show sympathy with this view. On the other hand, an investor who is exposed to a particular money yield will find that inflation has eroded the real purchasing power of the associated fixed money income amounts.

Redemption yield model

Consider a series of cash flows. In a general sense, each cash flow may occur at various points in time and be of varying magnitude. For fixed-income gilts, however, the future cash flows and their payment dates will be covenanted. The discounted cash flow (DCF) methodology allows for both the timing and the size of each cash flow by discounting at an appropriate rate (or rates) of interest to a common instant in time.

If we define m as the coupon payment mode (frequency) such that, for example:

$m = 1$ for annual coupon amounts

$= 2$ for semi-annual coupon amounts

$= 4$ for quarterly coupon amounts

$= 12$ for monthly coupon amounts

Figure 2.2   *Example of the cash flows from a fixed-income bond*

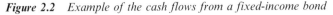

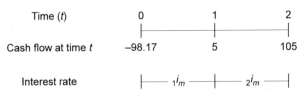

we can also define $_t i_m/m$ (in decimal form, or percentage form if multiplied by 100) as the effective rate of interest (or modal rate of interest) for the period $(t-1)/m$ to t/m (such that $t = 1, 2, \ldots$) convertible at time t/m. For example, Figure 2.2 represents the cash flows from a hypothetical fixed-income bond. If $m = 2$, so that coupon amounts are received twice yearly, and t measures time in half-yearly intervals, then a coupon amount of 5 is paid at the end of the first half-year (time $t = 1$) and $_1 i_2/2$ denotes the effective rate of interest applicable to the half-year period $t = 0$ to $t = 1$. A further coupon amount of 5 is also paid with a redemption amount of 100 at the end of one year (time $t = 2$) and $_2 i_2/2$ denotes the effective rate of interest applicable to the half-year period $t = 1$ to $t = 2$.

If the period between each coupon amount is of equal length, it is then useful to assume that the effective rate of interest has an effective period equal to that between coupon amounts (we can thus drop the subscript t in $_t i_m/m$). As a result, annualised or nominal rates of interest exist as some mode multiple of an effective rate of interest. If the effective period is $1/m^{\text{th}}$ fraction of a year and the effective rate of interest is i_m/m, then i_m is known as the annualised rate of interest (or nominal rate of interest over a year). In describing i_m, it is often offered with one of the terms 'convertible' or 'payable' monthly for $m = 12$; quarterly for $m = 4$; semi-annually for $m = 2$; annually for $m = 1$; or, more generally, every $1/m^{\text{th}}$ of a year. These expressions describe the number of times interest is converted in a year. For the example illustrated in Figure 2.2, if a cash flow occurs at the end of each equal length six-month period, then the analysis is often facilitated if the interest rate used to discount the cash flows is also convertible every six months. Each cash flow at time t would be discounted using the divisor $(1 + i_m/m)^t$ and then summed to total. (Used in this way, each i_m/m is colloquially termed an (effective) discount rate, although a discount rate can be defined differently. This terminology is derived from the expression $1/(1 + i_m/m)$ which is called a discount factor. Since this can be confusing, we shall continue to refer to i_m/m as an effective or modal rate of interest.)

Traditional gilt-edged stock involves the payment of fixed coupon amounts throughout a known life and a redemption amount on a future specified date, the redemption date or maturity date. (Our reference to 'gilt' or 'gilts' is specifically to that of fixed-income UK domestic government issued bonds in the rest of this book unless otherwise noted.) The outstanding period to maturity is referred to as a bond's *term to redemption, term to maturity*, or simply *term* (we use these expressions interchangeably with *life-to-maturity* or simply *life*, to refer to the outstanding life of a bond to its maturity date). (In practice, the date on which a bond transaction is agreed is called the *trade date* or *bargain date*. The date the transaction is to be settled is the *settlement date*. Throughout, unless noted otherwise, we make the simplifying assumption that both the standing and settlement dates are the same although in practice these will differ.) The coupon amounts are usually regular, although traditional gilt-edged stock may also have a shorter or longer first or last coupon pay date. Traditional gilt-edged stock has no other features, such as exchangeability, call options, put options, or sinking fund. It is with traditional gilt-edged stock that we shall be concerned in this book unless otherwise stated.

When a buyer and seller are attempting to agree on a price for a fixed-income bond, it is, of course, important that both sides understand the basis on which that trade may go ahead. A number of conventions have been established in the gilt market including the method of quotation, standard settlement and value date, method of accrued coupon adjustment, rounding and so on. Although we shall comment on specific market practice, comprehensive details of various bond market conventions and yield formulae are well covered in, for example, Brown (1998).

For a traditional gilt-edged stock, let us make the following simplifying assumptions.

1   Coupons are gross, fixed, regular amounts payable throughout a known life with each coupon payment occurring on a business day; redemption occurs by paying a fixed and known redemption amount on the same date as the final coupon payment. This also means the period between issue and the first coupon is of a normal coupon period length.
2   The period between each coupon pay date is comprised of an equal number of days.
3   All cash flows (coupon and redemption amount) are paid at the assumed times.
4   The bond is standing on a coupon pay-date (excluding that coupon).
5   The bond is held to its maturity date, and a present value only over the term to redemption of the bond is considered.
6   The nominal amount (that is, £100) of bond held remains constant throughout the term to maturity. This also means that no new bonds are added and there is no partial sale of existing bond, and neither is there a further payment due to the issuer (that is, the bond is fully-paid).
7   There are no tax, no dealing expenses and no other features.

These assumptions permit an easy DCF relationship for the present value:

$$\text{Present value} = \sum_{t=1}^{nc} C/m \times v_m{}^t + \text{RED} \times v_m{}^{nc}$$

where: $\sum$ = symbol for the sum of the discrete expression between $t = 1$ and $t = nc$;

t = number of coupon periods to each cash flow such that $t = 1, 2, \ldots, nc$;

C = the annualised coupon (per nominal amount of stock) payable in instalments of C/m every $1/m^{\text{th}}$ of a year (we will also refer to C/m as a modal coupon);

RED = redemption amount (per nominal amount of stock);

m = number of coupons payable in a complete year;

i_m = annualised rate of interest convertible m times a year (in decimal form);

i_m/m = modal (effective) rate of interest (in decimal form);

v_m = $1/(1 + i_m/m)$;

nc = number of future coupons payable to maturity (an integer multiple of m)

Since coupons for a traditional gilt-edged stock are assigned for payment on a particular date or dates each year, the assumption of an equal-length period between coupon pay dates (or the start date and the next coupon pay date) will often be unrealistic. The main reason for assuming equal-length coupon periods is that the equation of value for the present value then involves an immediate (payable in arrears) annuity of coupon payments which can be manipulated in a variety of ways to simplify the summation. Assuming intermediate rounding is not undertaken, one simplified form gives:

$$\text{Present value} = C \times (1 - v_m{}^{nc})/i_m + \text{RED} \times v_m{}^{nc}$$

The rate of interest, i_m, that capitalises the gross coupon payments and redemption amount on a traditional gilt-edged stock to its price is called the *gross redemption yield* (we shall also refer to this as simply *yield* or *redemption yield*).

With a redemption amount equal to the par (nominal) value, that is, 100, consider these relationships for a traditional gilt-edged stock standing on a coupon pay-date (excluding that coupon):

(a) If price = 100, then $i_m = C/100$. Therefore, if the coupon rate equals the gross redemption yield (convertible at the same mode as the coupons are payable), the bond can be said to be *trading at par*.

(b) If price > 100, then if $i_m < C/100$ the bond can be said to be trading at a *redemption premium*. Therefore, the bond can be said to be trading at a *premium to par* if its gross redemption yield (convertible at the same mode as the coupons are payable) is less than its coupon rate.

(c) If price < 100, then if $i_m > C/100$ the bond can be said to be trading at a *redemption discount*. Therefore, the bond can be said to be trading at a *discount to par* if its gross redemption yield (convertible at the same mode as the coupons) is greater than its coupon rate.

To summarise for a par redeemable traditional gilt-edged stock standing on a coupon pay-date (excluding that coupon):

If price $= 100$, there is neither a redemption premium or redemption
   discount;
If price < 100, there is a redemption discount; and
If price > 100, there is a redemption premium.

It is possible to relate this to the calculation of a *simple yield to maturity* that amortises a redemption premium or a redemption discount at a uniform rate over the term to maturity. However, there is a simple rate of interest that can be applied to the cash flow stream from a traditional gilt-edged stock to generate a present value from which the cash flow stream so discounted is replicated by amortising a redemption premium or a redemption discount in a non-uniform way. This interest rate is the gross redemption yield.

The effect of a gross redemption yield in amortising a redemption premium or a redemption discount is illustrated in Figure 2.3. With a traditional gilt-edged stock priced at par and standing on a coupon pay-date (excluding that coupon), the gross redemption yield will be equivalent to its simple yield to maturity. In other situations, the relationship is more complex because, in addition, simple yield to maturity excludes accrued coupon (see Brown, 1998), while the gross redemption yield is based on that price that includes accrued coupon.

Since each coupon amount is payable at different times, a buyer of a traditional gilt-edged stock that is 'cum-div' (that is, cum-coupon) will receive the entire next coupon. To ensure an equitable distribution of the next coupon when a traditional gilt-edged stock is sold, the seller is compensated in proportion to that coupon pay-period since the last coupon (both periods measured in terms of actual number of days). The buyer defrays this in the form of 'gross accrued interest' (that is, gross accrued coupon).

A traditional gilt-edged stock may also be traded 'ex-div' (that is, ex-coupon) between coupon pay dates. Where a traditional gilt-edged stock is ex-div, a buyer is not entitled to the next coupon. The seller receives the entire next coupon so will defray this inequity with an extra payment to the buyer in

Figure 2.3   *Example of how redemption premium and redemption discount changes (between coupon pay-dates, excluding those coupons) at an amortisation rate equal to redemption yield*

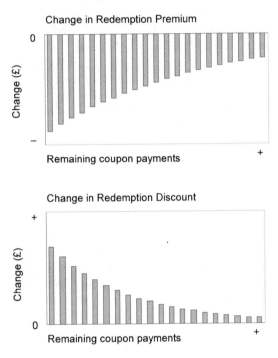

proportion to that coupon pay period to the next coupon payment date (both periods measured in terms of actual number of days).

Traditional gilt-edged stock prices that do not include accrued coupon are called clean prices. Therefore, the element of accrued coupon will be a part of the actual amount in cases where the quoted price is a clean price. The clean price plus any accrued coupon is known as the gross price and dubbed the 'dirty price' in market jargon (when we refer to a bond's price, it is the dirty price we mean in this book unless otherwise noted). In the traditional gilt-edged market, the yield would allow for any fractional coupon period and thus be based on the dirty price. Thus, while a cum-div traditional gilt would add the fractional coupon amount to the clean price, the accrued coupon for an ex-div gilt is also added to the clean price, so is calculated as a negative (that is, in effect it is deducted from the clean price). This means:

clean price ≥ dirty price for an ex-div traditional gilt-edged stock; and

clean price ≤ dirty price for a cum-div traditional gilt-edged stock.

In other markets, the convention or bond yield formula will vary. For example, US Treasury bonds do not trade ex-coupon. Even with traditional gilt-edged stock, model variations exist outside the formal market. One stockbroker determines gilt redemption yields that make allowance for the exact number days to each coupon amount (beyond that required for simply accrued coupon). This would aim to give a more accurate representation of the present value of the covenanted cash flows on a traditional gilt-edged stock. When a cash flow payment is delayed, this will have the effect of reducing the redemption yield. This can occur when the settlement date falls on a non-business day (this is the usual practice, although in some other markets this may be paid on the previous working day which will have the effect of increasing the resulting redemption yield since it brings a cash flow payment forward). Further, the convention with traditional gilt-edged stock is to determine an annualised rate convertible semi-annually, i_2 per cent. Where the resulting redemption yield is an annualised six-month rate it may be converted into an effective annual rate from the following compound interest relation (assuming each coupon period mode is of equal length and interest compounding at the semi-annual redemption yield):

$$(1 + i_2/2)^2 = 1 + i$$

where i and i_2 are in decimal form, so that

$$i\% = [1 + i_2/2)^2 - 1] \times 100$$

For example, suppose $i_2\% = 8\%$. The effective annual rate is:

$$
\begin{aligned}
i\% &= [(1 + 0.08/2)^2 - 1] \times 100 \\
&= 8.16\%
\end{aligned}
$$

Consider what happens to the present value of the cash flows between coupon pay-dates assuming a constant gross redemption yield. Immediately after a coupon amount has been paid, accrued coupon from the next coupon starts to build up in the present value. When this eventually falls out, the present value falls again and unless the loan has ceased, the process of accruing coupon from the next coupon amount starts again. The effect is that the present value profile to maturity for a constant redemption yield does not follow a smooth path. Of course, over an odd coupon pay-period, the modal gross redemption yield will also reflect a longer or shorter period, but the assumption of compounding of yield can be used to make comparison consistent over an equivalent period of time.

Holding period model

Suppose a traditional gilt-edged stock is not held to maturity. To determine the yield over the period held requires an estimate of the price at which the bond can be sold rather than the redemption amount the redemption yield assumes. The redemption yield is thus a specific example of a holding period yield.

Since the redemption yield considers both the timing and size of each cash flow, it can be viewed in the context of a normal rate of interest. One way this can be seen is to picture a hypothetical bank deposit account that runs in parallel with a traditional gilt-edged stock. Suppose the bond accumulated all its cash flows to maturity at a constant rate of interest. For the hypothetical deposit account to offer the same accumulated value at the same date, we can determine an initial deposit balance assuming no withdrawals or further deposits ahead of the maturity date. In this instance, if the rate of interest on the deposit balance must equal that used to accumulate the cash flows then the initial deposit balance would equal the present value of those cash flows at that cash flow accumulation rate. To see this more clearly, consider a hypothetical traditional gilt that is priced at £100 on a coupon pay-date (excluding that coupon) and paying £10 p.a. semi-annually with a redemption yield of 10 per cent p.a. semi-annual redeemable at £100 in 2 years' time. The future value of this bond at the maturity date if the redemption yield is assumed to be the coupon reinvestment rate is:

$$FV = 5 \times (1.05^{2 \times 2} - 1)/0.05 + 100$$
$$= £121.55 \text{ (rounded)}$$

The total rate of return earned on the investment is $[(121.55/100)^{1/4} - 1] \times 2 = 10$ per cent p.a. (rounded) convertible semi-annually, the same as the redemption yield.

The redemption yield reinvestment rate as an assumption also suggests that this bond will offer that yield on every assumed reinvestment date. However, if market yields change, the accumulated future value of this bond at the maturity date that was assumed in using a coupon reinvestment rate assumption equal to the redemption yield may not be achieved. Let us assume, for example, that it is possible to reinvest the coupons from this bond at only 9 per cent p.a. semi-annual. The estimated accumulated future value at maturity is given in Table 2.1, along with the value calculated above (ignoring rounding discrepancies).

The accumulated future value at maturity is therefore less at 9 per cent p.a. semi-annual than a 10 per cent p.a. semi-annual gross redemption yield reinvestment rate assumption would have suggested. One of the risks of assuming the redemption yield as a reinvestment rate to accumulate the cash

Table 2.1 *Accumulated future value at maturity of a 10 per cent p.a. semi-annual pay traditional bond using two different constant reinvestment rates of interest*

Time left to maturity	Coupon or RED	Effective interest assumption	Accumulated value at 10% p.a. semi-annual	Effective interest assumption	Accumulated value at 9% p.a. semi-annual
1.5 yrs	£5	5%	£5 $(1.05)^3$	4.5%	£5 $(1.045)^3$
1.0 yrs	£5	5%	£5 $(1.05)^2$	4.5%	£5 $(1.045)^2$
0.5 yrs	£5	5%	£5 (1.05)	4.5%	£5 (1.045)
0.0 yrs	£105		£105		£105
Total at maturity			£121.55		£121.39

Note: Figures have been rounded.

flows to maturity is therefore that the rate of interest earned on coupon reinvestment is different. The risk associated with achieving a different reinvestment rate than that expected or assumed (whether the redemption yield or other) is often called coupon reinvestment risk, or sometimes roll-up risk.

It is useful to break down the expected return to its constituent elements. To illustrate, let us continue with the previous example, assuming a 10 per cent p.a. semi-annual reinvestment rate:

Total coupon receipts:	£20.00
Coupon interest on interest:	£1.55
Gain/(loss) at maturity:	(0.00)
Total gain after two years (rounded to 2 d.p.)	£21.55

The total rate of return can then be estimated as $[1 + 21.55/100]^{1/4} - 1] \times 200$ = 10.00 per cent p.a. semi-annual (rounded), as before.

The above example also highlights the fact that the accumulated future value to maturity for a traditional gilt can be measured as the sum combination of three factors: the total coupon receipts; the interest on interest from the reinvestment of the intermediate coupons; and the gain or loss when the bond matures. Consider, for example, three hypothetical annual pay traditional bonds that are homogeneous except for coupon and standing on a coupon pay-date (excluding that coupon) and redeemable at par, with one standing at par, one standing at a discount to par and one standing at a premium to par. All three bonds are assumed to have the same term to maturity and the same redemption yield with coupon reinvestment at the same constant rate. In such situations, the bond least sensitive to coupon reinvestment will be found to be the discount bond. The bond most sensitive to coupon reinvestment will be found to be the premium bond. An example of the proportionate sources of return for three such bonds with 10-year maturities at a 10 per cent reinvestment rate assumption is given below:

Divergence to par	*Premium*	*Par*	*Discount*
Coupon receipts	67.05%	62.75%	57.23%
Interest on interest	39.8%	37.25%	33.98%
Maturity gain/(loss)	(6.87%)	0.00%	8.79%
Total	100%	100%	100%

Note: Figures rounded.

Some have criticised the redemption yield, arguing that as a coupon reinvestment rate it is an unlikely rate of interest and that, in addition, the holding period will not always correspond with the maturity date of a traditional gilt. As already highlighted, coupon reinvestment risk is a distinguishable consideration to redemption yield on a traditional gilt-edged stock. If the redemption yield remained constant over the term to maturity, then it would be possible to make reinvestment at that rate of interest. If, however, the reinvestment rate is above or below the redemption yield, the accumulated future cash flows will not equal a reinvestment rate assumption equal to redemption yield. It is also possible to make reinvestment at a lower rate of interest and other reinvestment at a higher rate of interest and still achieve an average reinvestment rate equal to redemption yield. However, as a freely trading asset, the yields on traditional gilt-edged stock will fluctuate in the market so that they may not move in a way that ensures attainment of a reinvestment rate equal to a traditional gilt-edged stock's redemption yield.

To say that a bond may be held over a period incongruous with maturity may be a valid comment, but the redemption yield is assumed to apply over the period to the maturity date of a traditional gilt-edged stock. The fault does not, therefore, lie with the method, but the assumptions made with a future cash flow stream over a period that is incongruous with some estimated holding period.

Other bond variations and features

Traditional gilt-edged stocks form one of the simplest fixed-income types. In practice, there are a number of bond variations, and traditional bonds may come with a number of different features. Some of these are touched on below.

An undated bond

This is analogous to a traditional stock but has a covenant to pay coupons forever (sometimes referred to as an irredeemable bond, although an irredeemable bond has also been defined simply as one that does not have an issuer call option or a holder put option). Two examples of undated (but callable) gilt-edged stock are 2½% Consols and 3½% Conversion Loan.

Undated with sinking fund

Although we are looking at the features and variations to a traditional bond one at a time, let us consider a specific example: the relative effect from a particular form of sinking fund.

At the time of writing, 3½% Conversion Loan had an interest yield of 3.97% and a price of 88.23. This gilt is similar to another undated gilt, 3½% War Loan, which had a calculated interest yield in excess of 4.59%. While both of these gilts have the same coupon rate, the difference in quoted yields is more than that which would be implied by simple differences in the payment date for the coupons.

The discrepancy in yield can be largely attributed to 3½% Conversion Loan, which is a little more difficult to assess since it also operates under a sinking fund. So long as the authorities have determined that the average price in the market over the current coupon pay period of this bond has been below 90, a proportion of the outstanding loan will be bought in the market over the next coupon pay period for cancellation. This sinking fund operates under a conditional bond price arrangement with a cancellation price determined in the market.

A variant sinking fund occurs when redemption of a proportion of an issue is covenanted to be on specified dates at a fixed redemption amount. In such instances, one approach to yield calculation is called the *yield-to-average-life*, or alternatively *yield-to-equivalent-life*, the latter having a term to equivalent life that allows for the present value of the repayments occurring at different points in time.

A zero-coupon bond (or pure discount bond)

This is analogous to a traditional bond but with zero coupons. There is therefore only a redemption amount.

With zero-coupon bonds, any question of coupon reinvestment is removed, so that they do not suffer from coupon reinvestment risk. However, some investors require a regular source of income while these issues provide no partial compensation (that would otherwise have been given through regular coupon payment) for future inflation during its life. For a corporate issuer, zero-coupon bonds obviate the need to service regular coupon payments and so help ease the cash flow servicing requirements on funding for a capital project during the phase where cash is being absorbed.

Callable bonds (sometimes referred to as double-dated or dual-dated bonds)

These bonds incorporate a call option that permits early redemption at the choice of the issuer. The call option usually begins some time after the bond was first issued (the call protection period) and exercise may be allowed on specified dates or may be continuous. The period during which a bond is redeemable is the *call period*. The price at which a bond can be redeemed at the choice of the issuer is the *call price*.

The conditions under which a bond may be redeemed by the issuer vary. Further, a bond that is callable will not necessarily entitle the holder to any accrued coupon since the last coupon payment if the issuer call option is exercised on a non-coupon pay date, that would depend on the issue terms and conditions. The decision to call a bond (as opposed to an issuer's right to call a bond) may be taken for a number of reasons, including:

- borrowings are still required, but it is cheaper to call the bond and refinance;
- the issuer has spare cash and thinks its own bonds offer a profitable place for that cash; or
- the conditions of the callable bond issue no longer suit the requirements of the issuer.

While a redemption yield can still be evaluated for callable bonds on the assumption that they will not be redeemed prior to maturity, callable bonds offer the possibility of accelerating the maturity date. While these are now more commonly viewed as a combination of a bond plus option, insights can be gauged by looking at them intuitively from the traditional approach, and it is this that we predominantly concentrate on here.

Given the price of a callable bond, it is possible to compare redemption yield and the yield if it were called. If the yield were calculated to all call dates (including the maturity date), the yield-to-worst forms the lowest resulting yield. Consider the equation of value for the present value of a traditional gilt-edged stock standing on a coupon pay-date (excluding that coupon) given earlier:

$$\text{Price} - \text{RED} = (C/i_m - \text{RED}) \times (1 - v_m{}^{nc})$$

Let us now assume this bond is callable only on a coupon pay-date (including the maturity date) with a fixed call price equal to the redemption amount. Then:

1   This bond will be standing at a price equal to its redemption amount if $C/RED = i_m$. Thus, when C/RED is equal to the redemption yield (convertible at the same mode as the coupons are payable), the redemption yield will equal that calculated to each of the subsequent coupon pay dates (excluding those coupons).

2   This bond will be standing at a premium to its redemption amount if $C/RED > i_m$. Thus, the redemption premium is realised early if the bond is redeemed prior to its maturity date. Since this accelerates the realisation of a gain, if C/RED is greater than the redemption yield (convertible at the same mode as the coupons are payable), the yield-to-next-call date will be less than the yield calculated to a coupon pay date (excluding that coupon) beyond the next call date (up to and including the maturity date). Thus, the yield-to-worst is the yield-to-next-call date.

    For example, a 15–year callable bond paying annual coupons of £10 semi-annually is priced at £114.43 on a coupon pay date (excluding that coupon) to yield 8.3 per cent p.a. semi-annual redeemable on each of the last five coupon pay-dates at its redemption amount of £100. Since the $C/RED = 10\%$ is greater than the redemption yield (convertible at the same mode as the coupons are payable), the yield-to-next at the given price will be greater than the yield calculated to a coupon pay-date (excluding that coupon) beyond the next call date. This occurs in ten years' time at £100.

3   This bond will be standing at a discount to its redemption amount if $C/RED < i_m$. Thus, the redemption discount is realised early if this bond is redeemed prior to maturity. Since this accelerates the realisation of a loss, if C/RED is less than the redemption yield (convertible at the same mode as the coupons are payable), the redemption yield will be less than the yield calculated to a coupon pay-date (excluding that coupon) prior to the maturity date. Thus, the yield-to-worst is the redemption yield.

    For example, a 10–year callable bond paying annual coupons of £10 semi-annually is priced at £94.31 on a coupon pay date (excluding that coupon) with a redemption yield of 10.95 per cent p.a. semi-annual redeemable on each of the last five coupon pay-dates at its redemption amount of £100. Since $C/RED = 10\%$ is less than the redemption yield (convertible at the same mode as the coupons are payable), the redemption yield at the given price will be less than the yield calculated to a coupon pay-date (excluding that coupon) prior to the maturity date.

The yield-to-worst will not necessarily be the earliest or latest possible call date when, for example, the call price is not the same on all the call dates (including the maturity date). In general, it may be necessary to apply a trial-and-error method on all possible call dates.

Callable bonds have been viewed increasingly as a synthetic combination of two elements: as a traditional bond (sometimes called the *bullet security*) and a call option. Thus, a traditional bond is bought and a call option is sold back to the issuer. The effect is that the issuer receives less and the buyer pays less than had an otherwise equivalent traditional bond been simply bought, reflecting the call option feature. The value of the call option is often estimated theoretically using probability-based valuation models (interested readers can find a discussion of embedded call options in Fabozzi, 1997, Ch. 36).

Puttable bonds

A traditional bond with a put-option contains provision for the bond to be redeemed early at a predetermined price (or prices) at a predetermined date (or dates) at the option of the holder. Normally, the first put date begins some time after the bond is first issued.

Viewed as a bond plus option, a bond that can be put offers the same rights and future benefits to the holder as an otherwise homogeneous traditional bond except one: the holder has an option to accelerate the maturity date. Given a bond's price, it is then possible to assess the effect of the put option. Consider, for example, a situation where the put price equals the redemption amount on all the put dates. Then, in general, the put becomes more valuable as the redemption yield rises and less valuable as the redemption yield declines.

Index-linked gilts: money yields

In theory, bonds can be indexed to almost any underlying property. In practice, they have been based predominantly on some measure of consumer prices. Even so, the design of index-linked bonds is not uniform across the various markets. In the next three sections, we shall specifically look at index-linked gilt-edged stock.

The Wilson Committee was established in the late 1970s to review the UK financial system. One of its many recommendations was for an assay with index-linked gilt-edged stock. The authorities duly made these available and although the original issues were available only to pension funds, this ownership restriction was removed in 1982.

These bonds link the coupons and the redemption amount (both established at outset) to the retail price index (RPI), lagged by eight months. For example, consider 2% Index-Linked Treasury Stock 1996. This was the first ever index-linked (IL) gilt, issued in March 1981, with coupons payable on 16 March and 16 September. The base RPI is that which applied to the eighth month prior to the issue month, so the base RPI is that for July 1980. The final coupon and the redemption proceeds became due on 16 September 1996 and were based on the RPI eight months earlier (that is, January 1996). The RPI adjustment over the life of this gilt is that which applied from July 1980 to January 1996. The 2 per cent is the outset coupon rate and is often called a 'real' coupon but, because of the RPI lagging, the inflation linking might differ from that over the actual calendar life of the gilt itself (we shall refer to the non-inflation adjusted initial coupon and redemption amount as outset cash flows). Further, the lagging of the RPI adjustment to the outset cash flows means an index-linked gilt can be viewed as a traditional fixed-income bond in the final eight months of its life since during this period there will be no further index-linking and thus the final two coupons and the maturity proceeds will be known in money terms.

While index-linked gilts are often held for reasons associated with (approximately) hedging future changes in the RPI, it should be recognised that the experienced inflation rate may be different. Final-salary-based pension funds, for example, have liabilities linked to salary inflation rather than retail price inflation and so it is important to recognise the limits of basing all future inflation assumptions on changes in the RPI alone.

The mechanics of indexing involve multiplying each outset cash flow (coupon and redemption amount) by the RPI that applied to the eighth month prior to that payment divided by the appropriate base RPI (say, RPI_0) to give the money cash flows. RPI_0 is fixed throughout the life of a particular gilt issue (although it may be rebased). For example, RPI_0 for 2% Index-Linked Treasury Stock 1996 was 67.91 after adjusting for the rebasing of the RPI to 100 in January 1987. The RPI applicable to the outset coupon payable on 16 September 1995 was 146.0, being the RPI for eight months before (that is, January 1995). The next semi-annual coupon was thus $146.0/67.91 \times £2/2 = £2.14$ (rounded down to 2 d.p. for this stock) per £100 of par value.

The rate of interest that discounts the money cash flows to the dirty price of an index-linked gilt is the money gross redemption yield (more often, it is known as a nominal redemption yield but we will not use this terminology since it can be confused with a nominal rate of interest). In determining the money redemption yield, a requirement is to forecast the future RPI values. There is no generally agreed way of doing this.

If the outset cash flows (coupons and redemption amount) at time t are denoted by CF_t, the next money cash flow will be worth $(RPI_1/RPI_0) \times CF_1$ where RPI_1 refers to the RPI value eight months prior to the CF_1 cash flow.

The subsequent money cash flows might be calculated by multiplying each outset cash flow by the ratio RPI_1/RPI_0 and then assuming an inflation rate from the date RPI_1 applies to eight months prior to each subsequent cash flow. There are obvious difficulties in estimating the inflation assumption for each future cash flow. The simplest assumption is to consider a constant (average) future compound rate of inflation. Incorporating this for an indexed-linked gilt standing on a coupon pay date (excluding that coupon):

$$\text{Present value} = (RPI_1/RPI_0) \times \sum_{t=1}^{nc} \frac{CF_t \times (1 + \inf_m/m)^{t-1}}{(1 + i_m/m)^t}$$

where: $\inf_m$ = constant annualised compound rate of RPI inflation assumption (convertible at the coupon mode, m-times per annum) from the date RPI_1 applies to eight months prior to each future outset cash flow $CF_{t>1}$

Since the RPI value corresponding to each cash flow payment date is unknown, one hypothesis is to assume that it is made the same number of days into the month as is the number of days into the month each cash flow is paid (clearly, a variety of possible assumptions can be made to allow for this; in practice, the assumption made here is probably the easiest). Under this assumption, let us denote the last published RPI by RPI_2, then consider the following relationship:

$$(RPI_2/RPI_0) \times (1 + \inf_m/m)^q$$

where: q = number of days from the month RPI_2 is calculated to the eighth month prior to the outset cash flow for which RPI_2 relates as a proportion of a normal coupon period

Taking the previous example, if the latest RPI known was for May 1995 ($= RPI_2$), q would refer to the period 16 May 1995 to 16 July 1995 and so would also allow for the RPI between 16 January 1995 and the latest published RPI. Thus, use is made of as much information as possible and the only inflation assumption required is for the period between the latest published RPI to eight months prior to maturity. Incorporating this in the equation of value gives:

$$\text{Present value} = (RPI_1/RPI_0) \times CF_1 \times v_m$$
$$+ (RPI_2/RPI_0) \times (1 + \inf_m/m)^q \times \sum_{t=2}^{nc} \frac{CF_t \times (1 + \inf_m/m)^{t-2}}{(1 + i_m/m)^t}$$

where: $\inf_m$ = constant annualised compound RPI inflation assumption (convertible at the coupon mode m times per annum) from the last published RPI (that is, RPI_2) to eight months prior to each future outset cash flow

While $\inf_m$ allows the money value of the outset cash flows to be determined, it will not be equal (except by chance) to the actual inflation rate experienced over the remaining *calendar life* of an index-linked gilt-edged stock. Further, more complicated assumptions about RPI inflation can be made, such as applying a varying RPI rate according to the time to each outset cash flow in an attempt to allow for the profile of future RPI inflation. However, it is common in the City of London for the redemption yield quoted on stockbrokers' daily price sheets to assume a constant rate of future inflation, and this is the simplistic approach we shall take in this book. Many also quote real yields.

Index-linked gilts: real yields

Traditional gilt-edged stocks suffer the prospect of future inflation diminishing the real value of the given money cash flows. For example, if inflation is 25 per cent over the year, a £1 coupon received in one year's time will then be worth only £0.80. As a result, future inflation is thought to have an important influence on fixed-income bond yields and therefore also on their prices (for a more detailed analysis of inflation and its variability on asset returns, see Corkish and Miles, 1994). Although we consider money yields, yield curves, spot rates and forward rates in this book, it is possible to derive, for each of these, a 'real' (inflation adjusted) equivalent (see Deacon and Derry, 1994). Below we deal with the notion of a real (RPI inflation adjusted) yield for index-linked gilts.

The money redemption yield for index-linked gilts, i_m, is often viewed as comprising two elements:

- RPI inflation; and
- a real redemption yield which makes allowance for the impact of RPI inflation.

Two approaches are often prescribed in deriving a real redemption yield: (i) calculate the money yield and deflate it by the assumed inflation rate; and (ii) convert the price into real (RPI inflation adjusted) terms (with an eight-month lag) and use the outset coupons and outset redemption amount to calculate the real yield (see Bootle, 1991, Appendix 1, for a reconciliation of the two methods). We shall consider the relationship between the money and real yield on the basis of a simplification that permits certain easy insights.

Therefore, let us assume the relationship between the real yield, r_m (an annualised rate convertible m times per annum), and its corresponding money yield over a complete equal-length coupon period for a constant assumed rate of inflation, $\inf_m$, gives:

$$(1 + r_m/m)(1 + \inf_m/m) = (1 + i_m/m)$$

or

$$(1 + r_m/m) = (1 + i_m/m)/(1 + \inf_m/m)$$

For example, assuming a 5 per cent p.a. effective inflation rate and a money yield of 8.827 per cent p.a. convertible semi-annually, the corresponding real yield using the above relationship is approximated as:

$$= [(1 + 0.08827/2)/1.05^{0.5} - 1] \times 200$$
$$= 3.79\% \text{ p.a. semi-annual (to 4 d.p.)}$$

Of course, inflation almost invariably fluctuates from period to period. Therefore, this measure provides for an additional simplification since it ignores the importance of the profile of inflation over a bond's life (see Bootle, 1991, Appendix 1). The significance of this is reinforced by a consideration of monetary policy where the Government has set an underlying inflation rate target that excludes the financing charges on a house mortgage (RPIX), but index-linked gilts are associated with a headline retail price index measure of inflation.

While the above offers a simple theoretical relationship between real yields and inflation, it is often thought to offer certain insights.

1   Under changing forecasts of the rate of inflation, what happens to the real yield? One theory is that this remains quite stable. However, a particular real yield presupposes a particular inflation assumption for any given money yield. To maintain the real yield, the ratio $(1 + i_m/m)/(1 + \inf_m/m)$ must remain constant as inflation rises or falls. The money yield, i_m, must therefore rise as inflation, $\inf_m$, rises, or fall as inflation falls to maintain a given real yield (that is, we are in some way back to Fisher's 1965 theory as set out in Brealey and Myers, 1996, Ch. 23). Nevertheless, if the future inflation rate is greater than that assumed, the real yield will be lower than that implicit in a given money yield, and if future inflation is less than that assumed, the real yield will be greater than that implicit in a given money yield. This highlights the need to forecast future inflation even when calculating real yields for any given money yield.

2   The real yield and the inflation rate are not simply additive since this would ignore the joint term associated with expanding the left-hand side of the money-yield relationship. This discrepancy will tend to increase as the real yield or inflation rate increase.

Index-linked gilts: break-even inflation rates

If the measure of inflation being priced into traditional gilt-edged stock by the market (on aggregate) is the expected future RPI inflation rate, then traditional gilts can also be broken down into the money and real (RPI adjusted) yield. However, there are differences between index-linked gilt-edged stock and traditional gilt-edged stock which means they can respond to different market pressures and offer different degrees of sensitivity to RPI adjustments. Considerations include the liquidity in each market and other risk premia and the taxation position of the respective participants in each market. The choice of traditional bond is therefore important (see Deacon and Derry, 1994). For our purposes, let us make the simplifying (theoretical) assumption that the same pressures apply to both markets. This information might then be used in the following way.

1   Select an appropriate traditional gilt-edged stock with similar character-istics, such as term to maturity, as the index-linked gilt.
2   Equate the market price of the index-linked gilt to its expected future money cash flows using an inflation rate that gives the same redemption yield as the selected traditional gilt.

To determine the inflation rate implicit in this approach usually requires the use of either iterative or trial-and-error methods. The resulting inflation rate is called the *break-even inflation rate*. For example, consider Table 2.2, which shows various real and money yields for two gilts assuming annual RPI inflation rates of 1 per cent, 2.76 per cent (break-even) and 5 per cent payable annually. At the break-even inflation rate, the money and real yield is the same for the two bonds. If RPI inflation is greater than the break-even inflation rate, the index-linked gilt has a higher money yield, because the money coupons increase, and a higher real yield. If the prospective inflation rate is below the break-even rate, the conventional gilt has a higher money yield since the money coupons remain constant while for the index-linked gilt the money coupons fall, although even here it is noteworthy that the real yield for the index-linked gilt rises as the future inflation rate falls.

The general gist of this analysis is that the real yield is more inflation-sensitive for traditional gilts than for index-linked gilts. If the future constant

Table 2.2 *Money and real yields for 2% index-linked 1996 and 10% conversion 1996*
for various RPI inflation rates at constant prices (%)

	GRY at an inflation rate assumption of:					
	1%	*1%*	*2.76%*	*2.76%*	*5%*	*5%*
	Money	*Real*	*Money*	*Real*	*Money*	*Real*
2% index-linked 1996	5.95	4.93	7.27	4.47	8.93	3.89
10% conversion 1996	7.27	6.24	7.27	4.47	7.27	2.27

Note: All figures rounded.

RPI inflation assumption is below the break-even rate, the traditional gilt will
implicitly offer a higher yield in real terms for any given money yield. If the
future constant RPI inflation assumption is greater than the break-even rate,
the index-linked gilt will implicitly offer a higher yield in real terms for any
given money yield. Some investors argue that the break-even inflation rate
reflects some kind of average (consensus) of the market's future RPI infla-
tionary expectation. While such theoretical arguments are often regarded as
being intuitive, the discussion by Deacon and Derry (1994) casts doubt over
the consensus inflation expectation argument because of the potential pro-
blem of distortion in the bonds utilised. However, they conclude that break-
even inflation rates can be useful in illustrating a time-series of how expectations have *changed*. It is also tempered by some historic observations (see
Frost and Hager, 1986).

1   Investments with a given future money cash flow stream may generally be
     preferred to those whose money cash flow stream is not covenanted in
     advance, such as index-linked gilts. Some investors have liabilities to meet
     that are determined in money terms, such as pure term (life) assurance
     that will usually be a fixed money amount. Others potentially face
     inflation adjustments to their income (or assets) and expenditure (or
     liabilities) that is related to some other measure of inflation and not the
     RPI such as insurers offering building insurance cover.
2   The UK tax system is still, at least in part, biased towards the money
     return rather than the real return.
3   Adjusted for the cost of living, real returns have been negative over past
     periods (for example, much of the late 1960s to the early 1970s), yet these
     effects do not seem to have tempered investors' requirement for tradi-
     tional gilts.

Estimates of the markets (on aggregate) expectation of future inflation
priced into future money coupons require a more sophisticated modelling
approach. This would deal with some of the distorting pressures discussed
earlier (see, for example, Deacon and Derry, 1994).

Other bond types and variations

A bond can be characterised according to a number of traits, including duration (discussed in Chapter 4). Simpler classifications involve reference to its coupon, its maturity and features. Traditional, zero coupon, irredeemable, callable and puttable bonds and index-linked gilts have already been discussed. Below is a brief description of some other types of bond.

Stripped bonds

These have their coupon payments and redemption amount separated (STRIPS is an acronym, although we will refer to these as 'strips' or a 'strip'). In effect, a stripped bond forms a series of zero-coupon bonds, where each represents a cash flow from a fixed-coupon bond. For example, a five-year semi-annual pay strippable traditional gilt could be separated into eleven zero-coupon bonds, ten from the semi-annual coupons (*coupon strips*) and one from the redemption amount (a *principal strip*). These strips can then be viewed and traded as separately issued bonds and are normally *fungible* (that is, they can be treated as homogeneous for any given maturity although in practice there are limitations to fungibility on principal strips in the UK gilts strips market).

Deep discount bonds (DDBs)

In simple terms, these are issued at a significant price below (or discount to) their redemption amount. A *stepped coupon bond* is a form of DDB, where the coupons rise in fixed steps at predefined points in time in the future from a low starting level.

Dual currency bonds

These pay coupons and the redemption amount in a currency other than that in which they are issued. The exchange rate is fixed throughout the life of these bonds.

Partly paid bonds

In contrast to a fully paid bond, the price of a partly paid bond is based on an initial part-payment with the balance payable in instalments. A partly paid fixed-income bond will have measured gearing to a change in its fully paid form. This aims to factor a response of the partly paid to a change in its fully paid form that reflects their relative prices.

Convertible bonds

These can describe a number of different types of bond. Equity convertible bonds are hybrids that also give the owner the option to convert into a given number of ordinary or preference shares of a company. The shares are usually those of the issuer of the convertible.

Some bonds are called convertible, but are really exchange bonds, which means that the bond can be exchanged for another, usually of a longer maturity. (Gilt-edged stocks with 'Conversion' in their title refer to stock converted from another issue: for example, 9% Conversion Stock 2000.) Other convertible bonds might have both the features of equity convertibility and exchangeability which may also involve a different coupon rate from the existing bond.

Medium-term notes

These developed as an extension of the commercial paper market and have initial lives that have ranged from a little under one year to many years. They can also offer a variety of features (for example, they may come with a put or call, or they may be issued with zero-coupons).

Variable coupon bonds

These are used to describe a variety of particular bond features. *Foreign currency bonds* have coupons that are payable in a currency that fluctuates with the currency of issue. *Floating rate notes*, also called variable rate bonds, are used in a very broad way in financial jargon. For example, these may pay coupons that are linked to some interbank rate, they may be perpetual or come with a fixed redemption date.

Other engineered structures and bond types

Although not necessarily issued under the guise of a bond, other arrangements involve many of the characteristics associated with bonds, both fixed and variable. Retractable or extendable bonds usually involve a finite life, but the coupon is re-fixed periodically which will normally include early repayment options (a put and a call) as an alternative to either party having to accept the re-fixing rate. Financial engineering aims to adapt an existing financial arrangement into one that is considered better suited. Examples include *forward rate agreements* (sometimes called a futures rate agreement, which should not be confused with financial futures), *reverse floating-rate notes* and *interest rate swaps* where a fixed-rate loan and a floating rate loan in the same currency are swapped without a physical exchange of principle (for an array of different exotic instruments, see, for example, Galitz, 1994).

General risk considerations

As we have already noted, models form a simplification of real world behaviour. In practice, further considerations are required. These are wide and varied, but some issues are outlined below.

1   Tax effects remain an important consideration for bond market partici-
    pants. Relevant changes in taxation can make a bond more, or less,
    attractive. Indeed, because market participants are likely to be operating
    in the markets under a variety of applicable tax arrangements, bond
    prices would tend to reflect the combination of these influences rather
    than any single demand influence that the gross redemption yield would
    suggest.
2   Liquidity risk (sometimes generically described as marketability risk) is a
    general term used to describe the extent of ease with which a trade can be
    fulfilled in the secondary markets. The extent to which a large sized trade
    can be fulfilled without unduly disturbing the current market price has
    been dubbed 'depth' in market jargon. Market access risk (sometimes
    called liquidity risk) refers to the drying-up of a firm's access to the
    financial markets. Companies often need to re-borrow, at times regularly
    where the length of time associated with a project exceeds the term of its
    initial financing arrangement. This can also affect whole economies such
    as Mexico in the mid-1990s, which suffered a liquidity crisis that was
    eventually resolved at that time with US support.
3   The potential exists for an expropriation of wealth from corporate
    bondholders. Bondholders and other interested parties, such as share-
    holders, have contrasting rights over a firm's cash flows. As a result,
    shareholders and bondholders can view a company's capital investment
    and dividend policy in a different way. Event risk arises, in the context of
    a bond, from an unforeseen event triggering a significant and precipitous
    fall in credit quality. This might, for example, arise from some integration
    activity or financial restructuring. Such action might not necessarily be
    adverse to the equity holders. To help protect corporate bondholders,
    protective covenants and other conditions might be written into a
    corporate bond's issue terms and conditions.

4   Default risk is also referred to as credit risk or, more broadly, counter party risk. Other forms of counter party risk also exist. For example, because financial transactions invariably involve more than one party, some practitioners recognise the default risk at the other end of a market buy or sell transaction itself. This involves counter party risk from the time a buy or sell transaction has been agreed to the time that all sides to that transaction settle (*settlement risk*). Although cash payment against delivery of a security's documentation can help to mitigate settlement risk, the potential for having to replace a failed transaction at less than otherwise advantageous terms to that of the original transaction is known as *replacement risk*.

5   Exchange rate risk involves the possibility of currency movements affecting the actual or expected return from owning a bond. This often occurs in cases where the price, coupons, or the redemption amount are paid in a different currency from that in which the expected return is being measured.

6   Some broader considerations include *political risk*, which relates to a country's willingness to honour its debt obligations on a timely basis, and to its commitment to an approximating *laissez-faire* doctrine for economic and capital markets. *Commodity price risk* is another category that relates to the effects of commodity inputs to the manufacturing process or an indirect effect, such as that on demand for a company's products, potentially affecting its ability to service current and future pecuniary obligations. Imponderables include a change in investor sentiment that is sometimes associated with an irrational market move, but can also relate to uncertainty.

References and further reading

Barr, D. G. and B. Pesaran (1995) *An assessment of the relative importance of real interest rates, inflation and term premia in determining the prices of real and nominal UK bonds*, Bank of England Working Paper Series No. 32 (April) (London: Bank of England).

Bootle, R. (1991) *Index-Linked Gilts (A Practical Guide)* (Cambridge: Woodhead-Faulkner).

Brealey, R. A. and S. C Myers (1996) *Principles of Corporate Finance*, 5th edn (London: McGraw-Hill).

Brown, P. (1998) *Bond Markets – Structures and Yield Calculations* (Cambridge/Edinburgh: International Securities Market Association (ISMA), in association with Globus Drummond Publishing).

Corkish, J. and D. Miles (1994) *Inflation, inflation risks and asset returns*, Bank of England Working Paper Series No. 27 (November) (London: Bank of England).

Deacon, M., and A. Derry (1994) *Deriving Estimates of Inflation Expectations from the Prices of UK Government Bonds*, Bank of England Working Paper Series No. 23 (July) (London: Bank of England).

Fabozzi, F. J. (editor) (1997) *The Handbook of Fixed Income Securities*, 5th edn (New York: McGraw-Hill)

Fisher, I. (1965) *The Theory of Interest: As Determined by Impatience to Spend Income and Opportunity to Invest* (New York: Augustus M. Kelley) (originally published 1930).

Frost, A. J. and D. P. Hager (1986) *A General Introduction to Institutional Investment* (London: Heinemann).

Galitz, L. (1994) *Financial Engineering* (London: Pitman).

UK Debt Management Office, *Gilt Review 1997—1998*, Her Majesty's Treasury (London: UK Debt Management Office).

3 Management Analysis of Gilt-Edged Stock

Reinvestment yield model

Let us assume that a rational investor is concerned with a five-year holding period and only has the following three mutually exclusive default-free traditional bonds as investment opportunities:

Bond	Coupon	Term to maturity (yrs)	Gross redemption yield
1	10	15	10.0%
2	8	5	9.9%
3	5	4	9.8%

This investor wants to assess which is likely to be the most profitable investment.

If bond 1 is purchased, the price at which it can be sold five years hence must be estimated because its term to maturity is greater than the expected holding period. Further, during the five-year holding period, it requires an estimate of the appropriate reinvestment rate for the coupons. This reinvestment rate need not necessarily turn out to equal that of the gross redemption yield.

Prima facie, bond 2 appears interesting because there is no need to estimate the price at which it can be sold five years hence, since it has a term to maturity equal to the holding period. However, this investor is still faced with deciding on the appropriate reinvestment rate for the coupons.

If bond 3 is purchased, at the end of year 4 it will be necessary to reinvest the realised accumulated future value for a further year to the end of the holding period. The total return after five years will then also depend on the one-year rate of interest beginning in four years' time that this investor is able to achieve on reinvesting the accumulated value to maturity.

The redemption yield and term to maturity are not proving very helpful measures to this investor. The most profitable choice depends on:

- the reinvestment rate(s) achieved on the coupons;
- the future price at the end of the holding period if the term to maturity of the bond is greater than the holding period;
- the reinvestment rate(s) on the realised accumulated future value to the end of the holding period if the term of the bond is less than the holding period.

44

Certain hypotheses as well as techniques may aid decision-making in bond analysis and one of these is the reinvestment yield model.

Reinvestment yields or balance-of-term yields (sometimes eloquently described as *riding the yield curve*) attempt to offer insights into a switch up or down the term to maturity spectrum of similar bonds. To see this as a simple example, consider two traditional gilt-edged stocks. One has a five-year maturity and the other a ten-year maturity. With an investment horizon of ten years, consider the following two choices:

(a) invest in the five-year bond and reinvest the estimated accumulated future value at the end of five years in another five-year bond;
(b) invest immediately in the ten-year bond.

It is then possible to determine the break-even price of the ten-year bond at the end of the five years at which reinvestment of the accumulated cash flows from the five-year bond leads to a break-even reinvestment rate of return. Value, however, is usually measured in terms of yield so that the ten-year bond's yield for the balance of term at the end of five years could be related to a forecast of its likely yield to offer additional insights.

Yield curves

Imagine a group of bonds that are homogeneous except for term to maturity. This means they are subject to the same forces of default, have no special features such as sinking fund or embedded option rights, and their market prices are not subject to distorting pressures such as taxation or liquidity. Further assume that there is at least one such bond at every point over a continuous lengthening of term to maturity. From such a group of bonds, the *yield curve* would represent a plot of redemption yield set against term to maturity.

The aim in generating a yield curve is to isolate gross redemption yield (some also look at net redemption yields at various assumed tax rates) as a sole function of term to maturity at a particular point in time (although some practitioners use 'modified duration' (see below) rather than term to maturity). Three of the more common generalised shapes include:

• a 'positively sloped' or 'upward sloping' yield curve, which occurs where the yield rises somewhat progressively as the maturity is lengthened;
• a 'negatively sloped', 'reverse', 'inverted', or 'downward sloping' yield curve, which is one where the yield falls somewhat progressively as the maturity is lengthened;
• a 'flat' yield curve, which occurs when the yield remains unchanged as the maturity is lengthened.

Figure 3.1 Examples of yield curve types

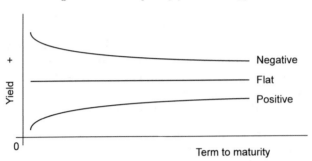

While the yield curve at any point in time is of a particular shape, it is clearly subject to dynamic forces so can take different shapes over time. Examples of these are illustrated in Figure 3.1.

The ideal yield curve would comprise a group of bonds that are homogeneous except for term to maturity. In practice, such a group of bonds does not exist, so a proxy group is used. The main proxy is usually taken from traditional gilt-edged stock trading in the market because there are many similar issues without distorting features such as sinking fund or call options in a market that is one of the more liquid. Of course, the full faith and credit from a single borrower (the UK Government) guarantees these bonds.

Traditional gilt-edged stocks have usually been issued near par, but this meant different issues needed different coupon rates. As a result, the coupon effect on different gilt yields and the redemption premium or redemption discount will vary between different issues trading in the market. In addition, different investors will value these bonds according to their own tax position (for a historical insight, see Derry and Pradham, 1993). Thus, when a yield curve is mathematically derived from market data, the underlying flow of the data will be represented even if there are data plots that deviate from the final smoothed curve (see Deacon and Derry, 1994, No. 24).

These considerations may be thought to limit the practical application of yield curve analysis. However, as the derivation of yield curves has become more sophisticated, and as the more recent changes to the gilt market have taken effect, there is evidence to suggest that the data plot deviations against the Bank of England's own yield curve model narrowed (see Bank of England, 1997). To facilitate decision-making, some investors simply make allowance for the historic yield deviation of an individual gilt against its yield curve taking into account the trend towards redemption. However, this approach also requires knowledge on what and how certain factors affect segments of the curve. For example, benchmark bonds will tend to trade relatively dearer than non-benchmark bonds at the relevant maturity. Other factors may be more permanent. Some investors approximate probabilities based on recent historical relations and relate these to the corresponding confidence intervals based on an assumption about the probability distribution of the relevant theoretical yield spread data points. Further, if fixed-income market participants on aggregate are good at forecasting the state of an economy, then the yield curve should provide useful information (see, for example, Deacon and Derry, 1994, No. 23).

Explaining the shape of the yield curve

An attempt to explain the shape of the yield curve has been expounded through a number of hypotheses. Two of the mainstream hypotheses are the expectation hypothesis and the market segmentation hypothesis. The former hypothesis has taken on various forms, but we shall discuss one of its conceptually easier forms in this section: the pure expectation hypothesis. The pure expectations hypothesis has itself been interpreted in various ways (reviewed in Fabozzi, 1997), but we will constrain what follows to that of the most specific of interpretations.

Pure expectations hypothesis

This hypothesis argues that the interest rate expectations of market participants form the sole determinant of the shape of the yield curve. If the activity of market participants is based purely on their expectations about future interest rates, then risk arbitrage arguments can be used to offer the hypothesis that consensus estimates of forward rates are implied in every yield curve. However, before going on to discuss forward rates, we need to know something about spot rates.

The redemption yield assumes the same interest rate is applicable to each cash flow, but the yield curve is rarely exactly flat. Spot rates, however, overcome this constraint and are helpful in offering insights into the static interest rate structure measured according to term to maturity (sometimes described as the *term-structure of interest rates*). A spot rate over a given time period can be defined as the (normally gross) redemption yield on a single end-period cash flow amount. The graph of the spot rate set against term to maturity taken from market information is known as the *spot rate curve*. To derive a continuous spot rate curve, spot rates are typically derived from mathematical arguments based on traditional coupon bonds trading in the market (see, for example, Deacon and Derry, 1994, No. 24). A plot of the derived spot-rates set against term to maturity gives a graph known as a *theoretical spot rate curve*.

The stripping of traditional gilt-edged stock allows the separation of each of the constituent cash flows to be traded as an independent bond. The ability to recreate these separate cash flows through the strips market might throw up a number of arbitrage trading strategies that would not otherwise be possible or obvious. Consider a bond that has a set of cash flows which can be replicated using a combination of zero-coupon bonds. If each zero-coupon cash flow is fungible (that is, homogeneous) with each of the corresponding bond's cash flows, the stripping or reconstituting (reconstructing) of those cash flows can offer a margin of arbitrage profit if differences exist. To remove such action, the present value of each cash flow from a traditional bond using the observed spot rates should sum to equal the price of that traditional bond. Since the redemption yield on a traditional gilt-edged stock would also have given the price (by definition), it follows that the redemption yield of a bond comprises a series of intervening rates of interest. The redemption yield itself is often argued to be some complex average rate comprising this set of intervening rates of interest. When traditional gilt-edged stocks are used to estimate spot rates, these intervening rates are the favoured quantified outcome to this theoretical arbitrage-free argument that generates the theoretical spot rates.

The more recent creation of a UK strips market means that a spot rate curve can, to some extent, now be observed. Table 3.1 lists the strippable gilts as at 31 March 1999.

In practice, demand and supply will determine a strip whilst a traditional gilt at every maturity point does not exist. Further, liquidity in the strips

Table 3.1 *Outstanding nominal value of strippable gilts and the proportions stripped as at 31 March 1999*

Name of stock and redemption month	Nominal amount outstanding (£ millions)	Proportion stripped
8% Treasury Stock 2000, December	9 800	1.27%
7% Treasury Stock 2002, June	9 000	2.69%
6½% Treasury Stock 2003, December	7 987	1.44%
8½% Treasury Stock 2005, December	10 373	4.71%
7½% Treasury Stock 2006, December	11 700	1.42%
7¼% Treasury Stock 2007, December	11 000	2.26%
5¾% Treasury 2009, December	6 277	1.29%
8% Treasury Stock 2015, December	13 787	1.52%
8% Treasury Stock 2021, June	16 500	2.95%
6% Treasury 2028, December	5 000	3.08%

Note: Proportions stripped are rounded percentage figures.
Source: UK Debt Management Office.

market is likely to differ relative to that on traditional government securities, and fungibility may be restricted or prevented (for example, on principal strips with implications for the yields these will trade at in the market relative to coupon strips of the same maturity). Therefore, yields from a theoretical spot rate curve and its corresponding strips curve may not be of identical shape when plotted against term to maturity (see the example in UK Debt Management Office, 1998, p. 39). These considerations mean that, in practice, the implications derived from a comparison of the zero-coupon curve with that of the theoretical spot rate curve is only indicative. However, let us continue with theory and assume these considerations are not an issue.

The redemption yield uses a single, constant rate of interest to discount a series of cash flows. However, two bonds that are homogeneous except for term to maturity may generally exhibit differences in redemption yield. Unless the yield curve is flat, this will result in a discounting of identical cash flows payable on the same date at different rates of interest; similarly, if the redemption yield is used as a coupon reinvestment rate assumption (see Day and Jamieson, 1984, Vol. II).

To see this, consider the following. A forward rate can be defined as the fixed rate of interest for lending over a fixed period of time that is deferred. The present value of a one-year pure discount bond yielding $_1s_0$ per cent p.a. (representing the immediately available one-year annual compound spot rate) is:

Present value $= \mathrm{RED}/(1 + {_1s_0})$

where $_1s_0$ is in decimal form. The present value of a two-year pure discount bond with a redemption yield of $_2s_0$ per cent p.a. (representing the immediately available two-year annual compound spot rate) taken from the same yield curve is:

Present value $= \mathrm{RED}/(1 + {_2s_0})^2$

where $_2s_0$ is in decimal form. With the redemption amounts equal, a consistent market implies there will be no economic difference between these choices if:

$$(1 + {_1s_0})(1 + {_1f_1}) = (1 + {_2s_0})^2$$

where $_1f_1$ is the implied one-year forward rate beginning in one year's time (in decimal form). With a market that is comprised of participants that have perfect forecasting ability, $_1f_1$ will be unambiguously determined. Participants would buy or sell $_1s_0$ against $_1f_1$ until the relationship reflects their equilibrium expectations. The pure expectation hypothesis argues that the (consensus market) forward rate for one year, starting in one year's time, should be equal to $_1f_1$.

It is possible to develop a term structure of forward rates using the simple reasoning above or a more complex form of analysis. Consider, for example, a traditional bond redeemable at £100 that pays coupons of £12 annually with three years to maturity, priced at £100.37 on a coupon pay-date (excluding that coupon) to yield 11.847 per cent p.a. effective. The one-year rate is 10 per cent p.a., and the theoretical expected one-year rate in one year's time is 12.009 per cent and the theoretical expected one-year rate in two years' time is 14.027 per cent. Discounting the cash flows from this bond using the implied forward rates should in theory give a present value equal to price; this calculation is illustrated in Table 3.2. The present value is determined by discounting each cash flow over each year at the appropriate forward rate and then adding it to the total. The total present value is:

Present value = 100.37

In using the redemption yield, the intermediate coupons from a traditional gilt-edged stock are discounted at the redemption yield. In the pure expectation hypothesis, the assumption is that the intermediate coupons from each bond can be discounted at the future implied spot rates. The future implied spot rates under the hypothesis would be derived as the implied forward rates in the term structure of interest rates.

Market segmentation hypothesis

The investment strategy of financial institutions would consider many aspects, including their tax position and asset and liability structure. Many of these institutions will have assets and liabilities that are interest rate sensitive and so might aim to align these assets in a way that reduces interest rate risk. These liabilities may conveniently be segmented according to their maturity, such as short-term or long-term, and the market segmentation hypothesis asserts that these institutions have preferences as to where their

Table 3.2   Example of the present value of the cash flows from a traditional annual-pay bond standing on a coupon pay-date (excluding that coupon) at the implied forward rates of interest

Year (t)	Forward rate symbol	Forward rate (%)	CFt	PV
1	$_1 f_0$	10.000	12	10.91
2	$_1 f_1$	12.009	12	9.74
3	$_1 f_2$	14.027	112	79.72
Total present value				100.37

Note: Figures rounded.

assets are positioned to better match their liabilities. The hypothesis argues that these institutions would not be prepared to mis-match their asset and liability profiles so leading to a lack of activity based on pure interest rate expectations between the preferred segments of the market.

Consider the composition of gilt holdings shown in Table 3.3. While a life assurance office will want to match liabilities that can be quantified, the growth of unit-linked life business over more recent years will have shifted the investment liability profile of that business more towards that of the policy-holder. Considering the issuance needs and preferences of the authorities, the supply of government debt will also play its role on the shape of the yield curve (a factor more prominent over recent years).

The pure expectation and market segmentation hypotheses are both intuitive. The purest form of expectation hypothesis argues that it is possible to derive expectations that assume away uncertainty. In practice, expectations are subject to uncertainty because of the possibility of materially relevant unanticipated events or a reassessment of past events. Barr and Pesaran (1995) empirically investigated the causes of unanticipated movements in the prices of real and nominal bonds from news about fundamentals (expected real interest and inflation rates) and expected future risk premia covering the period 1983–93. For conventional gilt-edged stock, they based their data on the Bank of England's par yield curve model. In the absence of a ten-year index-linked gilt, they derived a proxy using a composite based on two existing index-linked bonds on either side of the ten-year maturity point (while relatively less accurate, this reflected the market conditions faced by investors at that time). The measure of inflation used was the retail price index. They deduced that, amongst other significant factors, revisions to expected inflation were the dominant factor explaining unexpected move-ments in the prices of long-term conventional bonds over the study period.

Table 3.3 *Sectoral holdings of gilts (percentages) by market value*

	March 1999	March 1998	March 1997	March 1996
Insurance Companies and Pension Funds	63.6	64.4		
Life Assurance			57.1	53.2
Banks	4.8	6.7	8.3	7.5
Building societies	0.2	0.2	0.3	2.0
Other financial institutions	2.4	3.5	8.7	10.7
Public sector	1.1	0.8	0.8	0.8
Others	27.9	24.3	24.8	25.8

Source: Bank of England.

Therefore, recognising uncertainty, the implied forward rate structure and the future corresponding spot rates might not finish equal. However, this does not in itself invalidate the hypothesis that the theoretical forward rates were once aligned with the market's consensus view about the corresponding future spot rates. Market expectations might simply have reflected the information available at that time.

Duration and price volatility

Comparing one bond against another by term to maturity is hardly innovative. It suffers in many respects, and in particular it ignores the effect of different coupon rates. Introduced by Macaulay (1938), 'duration' (more technically known as the discounted mean term) provides an alternative:

$$\text{Duration (Macaulay) in years} = -\frac{1 + i_m/m}{\text{Price}} \times \frac{\partial \text{Price}}{\partial i_m}$$

where i_m is the bond's gross redemption yield. Macaulay duration uses the redemption yield (rather than the theoretical spot rates) for each cash flow maturity (we shall assume Macaulay duration in this book).

It is possible to show how duration varies with any particular factor, assuming the others are held constant, using mathematical methods. The duration calculation for a perpetual bond would cancel the coupon amounts from both the numerator and denominator so that duration becomes independent of coupon. In a world where all traditional bonds have the same coupon rate, redemption amount and gross redemption yield, duration will generally increase as term to maturity is lengthened (for some bonds, it is possible for duration to fall as term to maturity is lengthened). In a world where all traditional bonds have the same redemption amount, term to maturity and gross redemption yield, duration falls as the coupon rate rises and rises as the coupon rate falls. In a world where all traditional bonds have the same coupon rate, redemption amount and term to maturity duration falls as gross redemption yield rises and rises as gross redemption yield falls.

At the time of writing, the UK government benchmark yield curve exhibited a very steep upward slope for maturities between six months and two years. It was then humped between two- and ten-year maturities with a downward slope beyond the ten-year maturity. For this example, a plot of yield against duration or coupon rate against duration would highlight how these can vary across the curve. This is not surprising given that the coupon band of the benchmark bonds ranged from 5¾ per cent to 9 per cent and exhibited a gross redemption yield that varied from 4.71 per cent to 5.43 per cent. Thus duration is unlikely to be constant as maturity is lengthened along a yield curve, but the theorems of how duration varies with a particular factor as the others are held constant have been extended to a number of conceptual techniques. These include immunisation and (partial) price sensitivity to a change in yield.

Companies have both assets and liabilities. To the extent that assets are mis-matched to those factor influences affecting the liabilities, a company will be exposed to risk. Matching aims to establish an asset base that minimises the possibility of divergent responses by the liabilities to those common influences. In this general sense, matching might be related to a number of considerations including the influences from fluctuations in foreign exchange or inflation. In a more specific sense, immunisation involves establishing an efficient asset base in monetary terms that is equally responsive to the interest rate sensitivity of a set of monetary liabilities. While there are many different immunisation strategies, one of the simplest is formulated as a mathematical theory that allows the immunisation of a single, fixed liability amount payable at a known future time point to an immediate small change in a common yield.

Consider a simple example of interest rate immunisation that is concerned with the purpose of hedging interest rate risk. Suppose a company's treasury manager is told that the purchasing department will need £2 million in twenty days' time. There are many ways in which this can be handled. One possibility is to dedicate an amount of funds to meet the known future liability (a so-called *dedicated strategy*). This might result, for example, in the purchase of a single-coupon sterling Certificate of Deposit (CD) with a maturity value (face value plus coupon) of £2 million in twenty days' time (this example is analogous to purchasing a traditional gilt in its final coupon pay period). This of course assumes that the amount of money will not be required in less than twenty days (even if the CD is marketable, the market price could still be less than the required amount any time up to the twentieth day). In this way, the required amount will be available in twenty days, always assuming the CD issuer is able and willing to pay the face value and coupon. The required funds are thus immunised against changes in market interest rates since, at the maturity of the CD, £2 million will be available irrespective of interest rates in the intervening twenty-day period. In this situation, the asset duration was set equal to the single liability amount duration and forms one of the simplest duration-based strategies. It is also an example of a simple cash flow matching strategy where the timing and size of the asset cash inflow exactly matches the liability cash outflow requirement.

When an asset portfolio of different bonds is being used or when there is more than one liability amount to be immunised, Adams *et al.* (1993, Ch. 16) establish the more general conditions for immunisation in the case of an assumed small parallel shift in a common assets and liabilities yield rate. In many complex situations, the asset duration and the liability duration might have to be set up in such a way that they do not remain matched over time. This means the duration of the asset and the liability amount will need to be realigned. This process is known as *rebalancing* and must be carried out efficiently throughout the period of the liability to be efficacious. If it were possible to work out how the duration of the assets and the duration of the liabilities varied with continuous time, then it would be possible to better model both the initial immunisation position and the subsequent rebalancing process.

Consider the duration on a traditional gilt-edged stock. Duration is a dynamic measure that changes with the passage of time. For example, on an ex-div date the effect on duration will be a function of one less coupon. In some markets, bonds do not trade ex-div so the coupon adjustment to the duration measure occurs only on a coupon pay-date. Then, in the absence of a change in yield, Babcock (1986) asserts that duration will decline linearly between coupon pay-dates. This is because the weight in the duration measure represents the ratio of the present value of each cash flow to the price of the bond. He points out that these weights sum to one and will change only on a coupon pay date so that for an integer value of n outstanding coupon pay-periods and a change in time δt falling between coupon pay-dates:

$$\text{Dur}_{n-\delta t} = \text{Dur}_n - \delta t$$

where $\text{Dur}_n - \delta t = \sum^n weight \times (t - \delta t)$; $\text{Dur}_n = \sum^n weight \times t$; and *weight* is the present value of the cash flow at time t dividend by the bond's price. Similarly, if the numerator and denominator of the duration calculation for a traditional gilt-edged stock are adjusted for the relevant coupon pertaining to an ex-div date, then, in the absence of a change in yield, the resulting weights will have the same useful properties between ex-div dates.

The sensitivity of a traditional gilt-edged stock's price is often measured in relation to its redemption yield. By modifying duration, it becomes a partial measure of the relation between a traditional gilt-edged stock's change in price to a small change in its yield (the notion being introduced by Hicks, 1939). The change in yield is measured in basis points (where one basis point equals $1/100^{\text{th}}$ of 1 per cent which we will denote by 'bps' or 'bp'). However, before illustrating the relationship between duration and volatility, let us consider a more specific approach known as the *price value of a basis point* (PVBP) that gives the change in the cash price for a $1 - \text{bp}$ change in yield. It is given as:

$$\text{PVBP} = \text{Price} - \text{PV}'$$

where: Price uses the gross redemption yield; and
         PV′ uses the gross redemption yield plus or minus $1 - \text{bp}$

If the PVBP is divided by the price, the result is the percentage change in the price (if multiplied by 100, or otherwise in decimal form). This relationship can be used for any number of basis points (some like to work the other way round and determine the yield change to generate a given small change in price which is known as the *yield value of a price change*). For example, consider a 20-year traditional bond paying coupons of £10 semi-annually redeemable at £100, priced at £100 standing on a coupon pay-date (excluding that coupon) to yield 10 per cent p.a. semi-annual. The present value of this bond at various yields is:

Gross redemption yield	Present value
10.25%	£97.8913
10.0%	£100.0000
9.75%	£102.1821

Note: All figures rounded.

In each case, the absolute difference in yield from the 10 per cent rate is 25 bps. The change in the price from a redemption yield of 10 per cent to a redemption yield of 9.75 per cent is £102.1821 − £100 = £2.1821, and the percentage change is 2.1821 per cent. The change in the price from a redemption yield of 10 per cent to a yield of 10.25 per cent is £97.8913 − £100 = −£2.1087 and the percentage change is −2.1087 per cent. Comparing these results, it is easy to see that the price sensitivity is different for a 25 bp increase in the yield as compared to a 25 bp decrease.

A proportional measure of a price change for a small (one basis point) instantaneous change in redemption yield for a traditional gilt-edged stock is:

$$\frac{\text{Macaulay duration}}{(1 + i_m/m)}$$

This is known as *modified duration* (sometimes referred to simply as duration), although *price volatility* is also used in the UK (we shall denote this by Dmod). The graph of −Dmod multiplied by price (both at the redemption yield) as the gradient of the tangent of the price function of yield curve is depicted in Figure 3.2. Since Dmod extrapolates a linear estimate of a non-linear price function of yield, the error associated with Dmod increases the greater the change in yield being modelled. The error of approximation forms the difference between the Dmod tangent line and the price function of yield curve. If the change in gross redemption yield were a rise, the use of Dmod would result in the additive inverse to that of an equivalent fall in the gross redemption yield. For example, the approximate change in price of £100 for

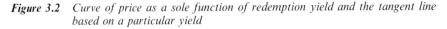

Figure 3.2   *Curve of price as a sole function of redemption yield and the tangent line based on a particular yield*

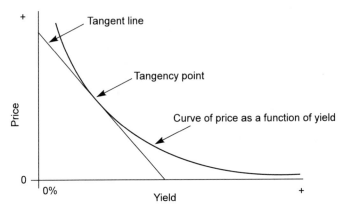

the previous example for an instantaneous 25 bp rise in gross redemption yield using Dmod can be measured as follows:

Duration	= 9.00852 years
Modified duration	= 9.00852/1.05
	= 8.57954,

so that:

Δ Price (approx.)	= −8.57954 × £100 × 0.25/100
	= −£2.1449 (rounded to 4 d.p.)

With a price of £100 the percentage change in the price is given approximately as −2.1449%. The actual change was previously calculated as −£2.1087 and the percentage change in price −2.1087 per cent. Modified duration would be incorrect by an absolute £0.0362 (or 3.62 per cent). With the Dmod calculation, a 25 bp fall in yield would result in the additive inverse for a 25 bp rise in yield, so the result would, again, be an approximation for the actual change in price. As the absolute change in yield gets smaller, the approximation error also gets smaller. Allied to the additive inverse property, these properties are used by managers of fixed-income bonds wanting a measure of the approximate responsiveness of their portfolio exposures to a small (in basis points) instantaneous change in yield without a necessary reference to the direction of that yield change.

Macaulay duration reflects a measure of price sensitivity to instantaneous and small (in basis points) uniform changes in yield. In other words, it is an

Figure 3.3   *The discount rate on three-month Treasury bills and yield on 2½% Consols*

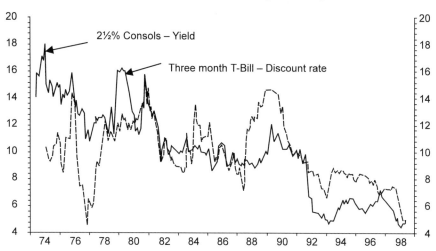

Source: Primark Datastream, reproduced with permission.

effect not a cause, so that yields can change by different amounts according to their term to maturity (described as a non-parallel shift in the yield curve). This will reflect many influences (see, for example, Dale, 1993). Therefore, relative theoretical price volatility does not mean that, for example, simply because three-month Treasury bills have a lower theoretical price volatility than 2½% Consols, the discount rate (or the yield equivalent) on the former will fluctuate less than the yield on the latter. This has been the case during much of the period since the mid-1970s. Visually, this is indicated in Figure 3.3.

The shape of the price graph plotted against its yield assuming all other things are constant means modified duration increases in error as the assumed change in yield increases. The degree of non-linearity in the curve is known as *convexity*. Thus, the approximate percentage change in the price of a traditional bond caused by absolute changes in yield (price volatility) can be improved by considering the additive effects of modified duration and convexity. For a traditional gilt-edged stock, convexity can be measured as the second derivative of the price formula with respect to yield divided by the price:

$$\text{Convexity} = \frac{1}{\text{Price}} \times \frac{\partial^2 \text{Price}}{\partial i_m^2}$$

where i_m = gross redemption yield.

For example, consider a traditional bond paying annual coupons of £10 redeemable at £100 in 10 years' time, standing on a coupon pay date (excluding that coupon) and priced at £106.4172 to yield 9 per cent p.a. effective to maturity. The price change for a 100 bp change in the redemption yield, given that its duration is 6.86273 years and its convexity is 54.90455 years, is estimated as follows:

Modified duration	$= 6.86273/1.09$
	$= 6.29608$
Approx. ΔPrice from Dmod	$= 106.4172 \times 6.29608 \times 0.01$
	$= 6.70011$
Approx. ΔPrice from convexity	$= (106.4172/2) \times 54.90455 \times 0.012$
	$= 0.292139$

Impact of modified duration and convexity for a:

	100 bps fall in yield	*100 bps rise in yield*
Modified duration effect	$= £6.70011$	$(£6.70011)$
Convexity effect	$= £0.29214$	$£0.29214$
Combined effect	$= £6.99225$	$(£6.40797)$
Price (before GRY change)	$= £106.417$	$£106.417$
Approx. price (after GRY change)	$= £113.41$	$£100.01$

Note: All figures rounded.

The present value of this bond at a yield of 8 per cent is £113.42; at a yield of 10 per cent, the present value is £100. Thus, modified duration provides an initial approximation and convexity further reduces the approximation difference (extensions can be derived that account for the balance of the approximation difference). For traditional gilt-edged stock, convexity will always be positive (some bonds, such as those that are callable, can offer *negative convexity*: see, for example, Fabozzi, 1997, Ch. 5).

Therefore, actual return volatility needs to consider both the extent of yield change and price sensitivity to that yield change. Further, when considering yield changes beyond that of an instant in time (for example, one month) the effect of accrued coupon needs to be considered. For example, Anderson and Breedon (1996) looked at, amongst other asset classes, the return volatility (standard deviation) of three-month Treasury bills and a series of ten-year gilt-edged bonds. Using daily data from January 1979 (T-bills) and January

1980 (bonds, excluding accrued coupon) to August 1995 and monthly return data over the period February 1946 to August 1995, their results showed that the return volatility on gilts was greater than that for Treasury bills.

While financial institutions might be more willing to mis-match assets and liabilities according to the allure of available investment opportunities, this will reflect considerations such as the strength of their capital and reserve base and the size of their surplus. In a positive yield curve environment, yield will increase as maturity is lengthened. The importance of each facet will vary, but with part of the liability base of some financial institutions short-dated, it is then possible for these institutions to achieve a higher margin of yield spread by investing in longer dated government debt securities. Further, the effect from lengthening and the resulting yield pick-up will reflect the magnitude of lengthening and the steepness of the yield curve. For example, as a positive yield curve steepens above a yield, duration would be lower than it would otherwise have been for any unit lengthening of maturity. Although a relatively safer proposition is to match term to maturity of the investment with the expected holding period, it nevertheless will involve uncertainty for these institutions because of the resulting mis-match of assets and liabilities.

Active fixed-income fund managers might take positions based on their expectations about the directional movement or reshaping of the yield curve. For example, if yields go uniformly lower in a flat yield curve environment, then the attributes of high modified-duration (to increases the relative yield sensitivity of a portfolio) become relevant (see Figure 3.4). In general, considerations include low coupon, long maturity and high modified-duration. If yields go uniformly higher in a flat yield curve environment, then the converse attributes of low modified-duration (to reduce the relative yield sensitivity of a portfolio) become relevant (see Figure 3.4). In general, considerations include high coupon, short maturity and low modified-duration.

Figure 3.4   *A parallel shift of a flat yield curve*

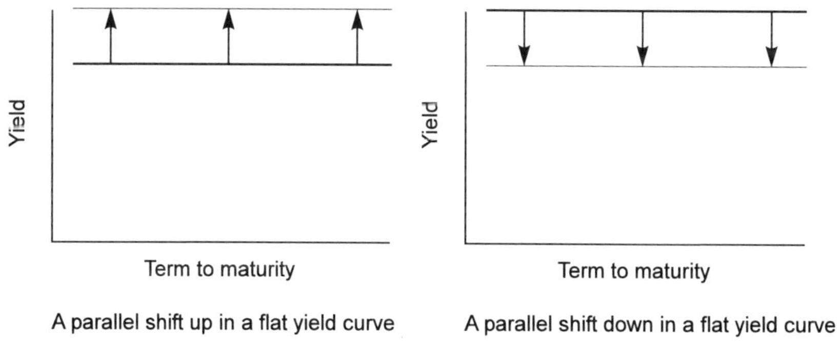

A parallel shift up in a flat yield curve   A parallel shift down in a flat yield curve

In practice, the motive-force behind a bond transaction is myriad. A bond switch is usually initiated because of an expectation that another bond will outperform, either for stock specific reasons or because of a broader market readjustment. A switch will thus involve judgement. To offer insights into the potential risk and reward from a switch, some investors look at price ratios on two similar bonds, one putative argument being that a plot of the historic price ratio over time may help to isolate deviations from the historic mean reverting (that is, reverting towards some historic mean from extremes) price ratio trend. This will involve many considerations in practice, including the potential risk of a historic price ratio fluctuating around a new level (rather than reverting to the mean), associated switch-related expenses, the impact from differences in coupon rate, ex-div dates and relative drift to the maturity date of each bond. An alternative is a yield-spread switch.

The negative correlation between a change in yield and a change in a traditional gilt-edged stock's price means yield-related measures are often thought to make isolating potential anomaly switches more obvious. The typical yield spread approach is to look for an anomalous yield pick-up and switch in the expectation of a yield spread convergence. Since redemption yields consider both the size and timing of cash flow payments, they help overcome one of the limitations associated with price ratios. However, yield spreads do not model the potential relative price sensitivity to changes in yield. Thus, a yield pick-up switch may or may not result in a relative total rate of return pick-up.

An analysis can be carried out to help offer insights into a yield pick-up switch between two similar gilts with differences in price leverage to changes in yield. These can involve complex mathematical and statistical methods or simple profit and loss scenarios that are quantified based on a forecast of the expected yield spread movements. The simplest specific situation occurs where the two bonds allow the determination of a break-even point at which the switch generates a break-even return for any given switch period. For example, consider the two hypothetical traditional bonds in Table 3.4.

Table 3.4 *Statistics on two hypothetical traditional bonds*

	Coupon rate (%)	*Term to maturity (yrs)*	*Gross redemption yield (%)*	*Price*
Bond 1	9	7	9.0	£100
Bond 2	9	6	9.3	£98⅔
Yield spread			0.3%	

Table 3.5 *Break-even yields at the end of a two-month switch period*

	Present value	Break-even yield (%)	Return (%)
Bond 1	£114.10	6.64	14.10
Bond 2	£112.57	6.64	14.10
Spreads		0.00	0.00

Note: All figures rounded.

While these bonds have different maturity dates, they are otherwise homogeneous. For example, they have the same credit risk, coupon payments payable at identical points in time and equal redemption amounts. Bond 1 also has a higher (modified) duration than bond 2. If bond 1 was sold in favour of bond 2, a yield pick-up of 30 bps is obtained. Now suppose the expectation is that at the end of two months, the yield pick-up would be removed by market moves. The break-even yield is shown in Table 3.5.

At the end of the two-month holding period, a yield below the break-even will result in bond 1 outperforming; a yield above the break-even will result in bond 2 outperforming. This is illustrated in Figure 3.5. Therefore, in this situation, the expectation of where the yield spread will eventually converge to a whole range of possible switch periods can be related to each corresponding break-even yield to offer additional insights into the risks of a yield spread convergence switch.

Figure 3.5 *Example of a break-even yield*

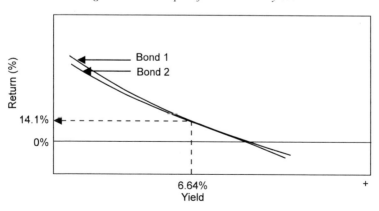

References and further reading

Adams, A., D. Bloomfield, P. Booth and P. England (1993) *Investment Mathematics and Statistics* (London: Graham & Trotman (Kluwer Academic Publishers Group)).

Anderson, N. and F. Breedon (1996) *UK Asset Price Volatility Over the Last 50 Years*, Bank of England Working Paper Series No. 51 (June) (London: Bank of England).

Babcock, G. C. (1986), 'On the Linearity of Duration', *Financial Analysts Journal* (Sept.–Oct.), pp. 75–7 (Charlottesville, Virginia: University of Chicago Press).

Bank of England (1997) *Gilts and the Gilt Market: Review 1996–1997* (31 March) (London: Bank of England).

Barr, D. G. and B. Pesaran (1995) *An Assessment of the Relative Importance of Real Interest Rates, Inflation and Term Premia in Determining the Prices of Real and Nominal UK Bonds*, Bank of England Working Paper Series No. 32 (April) (London: Bank of England).

Brown, P. (1998) *Bond Markets – Structures and Yield Calculations* (London/Cambridge, England: International Securities Market Association (ISMA) in association with Globus Drummond Publishing).

Dale, S. (1993) *The Effect of Official Interest Rate Changes on Market Rates since 1987*, Bank of England Working Paper Series No. 10 (April) (London: Bank of England).

Day, J. G. and A. T. Jamieson (1984) *Institutional Investment*, Volumes I–VI (London and Edinburgh: Institute of Actuaries and Faculty of Actuaries).

Deacon, M. and A. Derry (1994) *Deriving Estimates of Inflation Expectations from the Prices of UK Government Bonds*, Bank of England Working Paper Series No. 23 (July) (London: Bank of England).

Deacon, M. and A. Derry (1994) *Estimating the Term Structure of Interest Rates*, Bank of England Working Paper Series No. 24 (July) (London: Bank of England).

Derry, A. and M. Pradham (1993) *Tax Specific Term Structures of Interest Rates in the UK Government Bond Market*, Bank of England Working Paper series No. 11 (April) (London: Bank of England).

Fabozzi, F. J. (editor) (1997), *The Handbook of Fixed Income Securities*, 5th edn (New York: McGraw-Hill).

Galitz, L. (1995) *Financial Engineering* (London: Pitman).

Hicks, J. R. (1939) *Value and Capital: An Inquiry into Some Fundamental Principles of Economic Theory* (Oxford: Clarendon Press).

Macaulay, F. (1938) *Some Theoretical Problems Suggested by the Movements of Interest Rates, Bond Yields and Stock prices in the United States since 1865* (National Bureau of Economic Research).

UK Debt Management Office, *Gilt Review 1997–1998*, Her Majesty's Treasury (London).

Part III

Equity Securities

4 Portfolio Approaches and Company Analysis

Fundamental analysis

The sensitivity of different fundamental share return drivers will vary across industries. Fund managers look at a range of these drivers, but their focus tends to be somewhat different according to their approach to equity portfolio construction. This is illustrated in Figure 4.1. Managers of true index funds aggregate their holdings to reproduce their market index and thus aim to reproduce both the standard deviation and return of their chosen index. 'Top-down' fund managers apply an approach that is often based on the influence of macro-economic factors on a sector or industry and thus the individual equity holdings in a fund (we shall use the expression 'equity' and ordinary shares, or just 'shares', as interchangeable in this book). For example, one theory asserts that the investment implications might be discerned by investigating the relation between an industry's business cycle and the economic cycle. This economic cycle model of stock market behaviour is sometimes used in a broad fashion to justify the notion of sector rotation (changing the sector bias in a portfolio). Because each economic cycle will usually be different from that of another, this approach can lead to a changing profile of sector rotation over different cycles. To the extent that such themes may at times be less responsive to other sector rotation influences (for example, valuations), some active fund managers also aim to control and integrate other arguments into their overall investment decision.

The equity performance of an industry is thought to reflect a number of industry considerations. A stock market sector is defined by a common set of those industry considerations (there being differences between the definition preferences of a sector by many UK and US fund managers). In contrast, a 'bottom up' fund manager would focus predominantly on an individual

Figure 4.1   *Approaches to the equity portfolio construction decision*

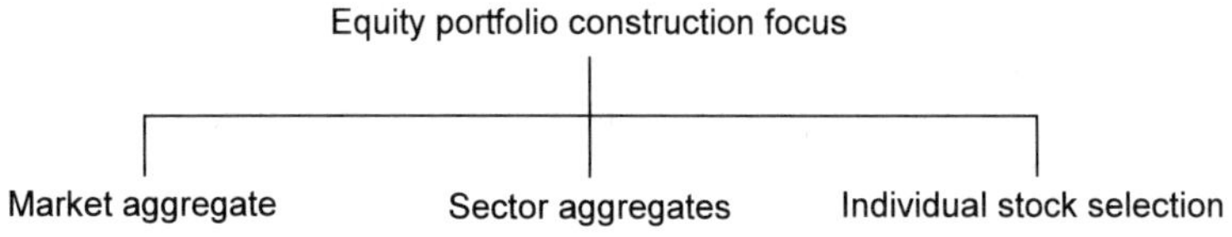

Equity portfolio construction focus

Market aggregate   Sector aggregates   Individual stock selection

equity. However, the bottom-up approach to sector selection may aggregate individual company variables, such as earnings, over the sector constituents before deciding on the final sector element of a portfolio. A more specific case of the bottom-up approach is that of the 'stock picker' who regards the individual selection of equities as the preferred way to construct a portfolio since a company's prospects may still differ relative to the outlook for its sector or industry. In the construction of an equity portfolio, stock pickers will tend to allocate funds across different sectors more directly from individual company analysis rather than as part of a conscious decision-making process, as in the top-down approach.

We can contrast fundamental analysis with traditional technical analysis, with the latter attempting to assess future share price movements by investigating historic price patterns and the market's buying and selling trends. Some fundamental based fund managers use technical analysis to help time a market action. Quantitative techniques are sometimes taken as being technical, and while we shall look at a number of quantitative relationships in later chapters, the traditional analysis of interpreting graphical trading patterns forms a specialist element of security analysis that is beyond the scope of this book.

Company objectives

Profit maximisation might be thought to be a suitable objective of a commercially motivated company. Since the ultimate owners of a listed company are its ordinary shareholders who place a value on their company in terms of the market price of its issued ordinary shares, that price is, among other things, usually related to a company's profits (or losses). However, profit itself needs to be priced. Total profit and profits per share are related but distinguishable measures. Since per share is the standardised measure of an equity shareholder's proportionate rights, then total profit becomes less important than profit per share. Even maximising profit per share can be argued to be a rather myopic objective of a company, for a number of reasons.

1   It ignores the timing and length of the future profit stream. For example, consider the net present value (NPV) of an investment in a capital project that will generate £5 million p.a. for five years and another project that will generate £3 million p.a. for ten years. The discounted present value at various rates of interest is illustrated in Figure 4.2. The net present value of each project will depend upon the rate of interest used for discounting and the size and timing of the amounts involved in each project.

Figure 4.2 *The NPV of £3 million p.a. for ten years and £5 million p.a. for five years discounted at various rates of interest*

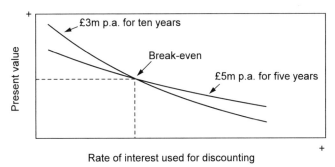

Rate of interest used for discounting

2   It ignores the risks of generating a profit stream. A project whose future profit stream can be ascertained exactly is less risky than one whose profit stream may show widely divergent patterns over time. In this way, different capital projects in the same industry can involve different levels of risk, as can projects across different industries. These risks might be perceived to increase as the amounts involved in a project rise relative to some measure of the existing size of a company. Thus the degree of debt financing relative to some measure of a company's capital or asset base, as well as the level of service costs of debt contracted by a business relative to its pre-interest profit or cash flow might also add to risk; taken together, financial considerations such as these are often termed *financial risk*.

3   There are many other considerations associated with profit. Principally, these involve defining and measuring profit unambiguously. For example, let us define profit simply as the excess of a company's value at the end of a year over that at the beginning after allowing for the costs consumed during the year. Some argue that these costs should include inflation. A company with assets worth £100 at the start of a year, and which earns and retains £20 of money profits over that year, may be said to have assets worth £120 at the end of that year. But with a general level of inflation, the value of its assets might be adjusted to take account of its effects, so the profit might, for example, be described as £10 to reflect the 'real' (inflation adjusted) wealth creation during the year (those interested in the historical impact of inflation on the prosperity of an economy can find a succinct description in two *Financial Times* articles: 'Elusive case for stable prices' and 'Price stability is the path to prosperity', dated 18 and 19 May 1995, respectively).

In the UK, the inflation adjustment has involved some average measure of inflation (as in current purchasing power accounting in the 1970s), or a more complex measure which attempted to make adjustments that were more specific (as in current cost accounting in the 1980s). Current cost accounting was not really satisfactory, partly because of its complexity, and was eventually superseded as inflation abated at that time. For the present, most UK financial statements are produced under the historic cost accounting approach, which generally ignores the impact of inflation, but may be modified to include certain assets at some revaluation.

4   Related dimensions also need to be considered. Cash flow not utilised in supporting existing operations is one funding source used to invest in new and ongoing capital projects and repay debt. Therefore, long-term cash flow is one measure of a company's capacity to invest in new projects. Extending this is the notion of return. If a company has a capacity to invest in new projects, then it must also position itself to generate a return from that investment. Further, strategic business decisions also need to be considered, since enhancing value through cash flow, profits or earnings, assets and returns can only be seen in the context of their quality.

For these and other reasons, profit (or earnings) maximisation is not necessarily consistent with the objective of maximising the value of a business to its ultimate owners. One view argues that this has to be balanced by the wide number of other responsibilities and obligations faced by many companies. These include employment issues as well as a number of other considerations, both internally and externally. Thus, creating value has been subject to disagreement about whose value ought to be maximised primarily centred on that between shareholders and the company itself (that would include all those to which the company has a fiduciary responsibility).

However, what is the empirical evidence? Bughin and Copeland (1997) and Copeland (1994) argue that a corporate focus on shareholder value maximisation leads to a long-term objective that need not be at the long-term expense of other company stakeholders. For instance, Bughin and Copeland (1997) offer empirical examples where long-term job creation was associated with measures of shareholder value. At the individual company level, they looked at examples from the Belgian market and found a link between employment growth and measures of value (according to market/book or market value increase) where each company was investigated over a period that ranged between the mid-1980s and 1995. At the country level, they looked at Germany, the Netherlands, Belgium, France, the USA and Canada over the period 1970 to 1990. They compared the USA and Canada against Europe and found that a decline in employment in continental Europe was linked to a negative shareholder spread measure of value.

Industry anaysis

Industry analysis aims to highlight broad industry trends that may offer insights into both the risks and the opportunities for an industry participant. Two considerations relate to the life cycle hypothesis and the competitive forces affecting an industry.

An industry may be at various stages of its life cycle (see Figure 4.3). (Note: Porter, 1980 points out that there is some controversy as to whether this applies to goods or to whole industries, although we shall not make such a distinction for the sake of simplicity.) This framework appears to have some analogy with the theory predicting the evolution of a species. However, Glucksman and Morecroft (1998) point out that an evolving species is only reactive to events while business managers 'have a degree of control over their environment and can develop insight into how it is evolving' (see also Chapter 8).

The four stages of development highlighted in Figure 4.3 involve the following.

1   *Introductory Stage* This occurs with the introduction of a product and is usually characterised by factors such as overcapacity and a low number of market participants.
2   *Growth Stage* This occurs when the demand for an industry's output is growing because of the impact on it by long-term forces.
3   *Mature Stage* This occurs where growth trends are low but demand patterns reasonably stable. These situations are often characterised by high entry costs relative to the potential returns. Some mature industries

Figure 4.3   *Stages of the life cycle*

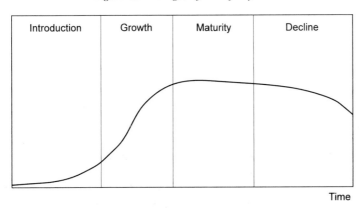

Note: Based on a work by Porter (1980) © The Free Press, reproduced with permission.

already have the structures in place to meet the needs of their market so earnings and cash flow tend to be relatively less affected by the need for additional capital expenditures.

4   *Declining Stage* This occurs in situations where an industry is in secular decline.

Not all industries will evolve in the same way. The time a particular industry spends in each stage of development may be different from that of another. Bypassing a stage is not unknown (see Porter, 1980, p. 158) and an industry can also revert from a stage as buyer purchasing reverses a previous trend (see, for example, the description of the development of the US semiconductor industry in Nevens, Guiniven and Paulsen, 1998). Some industries can enter a stage for transitory reasons. Government policy might, for example, give a short-term boost to an industry that is unsustainable over longer periods.

As an example, Nevens, Guiniven and Paulsen (1998) looked at electronics companies in the USA over the period 1983–96 for which at least five years' financial data were available. The framework they used was a three-stage product life cycle. In the first stage, technology allows the introduction of a product and market penetration is emphasised. In the second stage, the emphasis moves on to a greater balance between growth and profit. The third stage objective manages a business with an even greater emphasis on profit in a mature market. Their empirical analysis investigated correlated relations to stock market total returns to shareholders. Over the study period, they found that workstation manufacturers had the greatest correlation with revenue growth, semiconductor manufacturers were linked to current profitability and data communication companies were linked to both growth and profit.

Stock pickers recognise that although industries can be categorised as growth, mature, or declining, companies might be sub-classified. For example, a company may have exposure to overseas markets that are growing rapidly and so may not be classified as mature, like its domestic industry. Thus while it may be possible to classify industries as being in a growth, mature or declining stage, it does not always follow that every market participant of an industry should be classified in the same way. Nevertheless, the demand for many industries' output will tend to grow as aggregate demand in an economy is growing, and decline as aggregate demand in an economy is declining. Some industries are described as *cyclical* because of their high sensitivity to demand for the industry's output over an economic cycle (although some researchers define a cyclical stock as any that is more volatile than the stock market). The degree of responsiveness may occur with leads or lags. Other industries (for example, growth industries) might slow or even reverse previous trends under unfavourable economic conditions, although true growth industries will tend to exhibit such a phenomenon in the short term.

Figure 4.4   *Competitive structure of an industry*

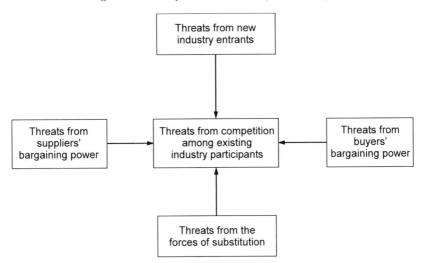

Note: Based on the schema by Porter (1980, p. 4), The Free Press, reproduced with permission.

Other considerations that can affect the outlook of a company include the changing internal forces affecting its industry and its competitive advantage therein. Figure 4.4 illustrates a schematic approach to appreciate the forces driving competition in an industry.

This schema highlights the fact that an industry is faced with different competitive pressures: from its suppliers and/or its buyers; by the threat of potential substitute products for those it sells; by the potential threat of new competitors entering an industry; and by an intensification of existing market competition. In this way the effect of a competitive market structure will be reflected in the balance of power to influence prices or volumes in an industry to the benefit or detriment of particular market participants, or the industry overall. It also highlights the importance of a company's dependence on the well-being of its suppliers and buyers.

It is often difficult to assess when the transition from one life cycle stage into another is occurring but as the life cycle develops corporate management face the challenge of adapting their business model to the potential new economics. In the study by Nevens, Guiniven and Paulsen (1998), early results on the US electronics industry suggest that there were changing strategic requirements over relatively short periods of time. More conventionally, to appreciate the possible implications for an individual company within an industry requires an assessment of those forces driving competition, including the following.

1   The nature of competition, such as government and regulatory policy, product differentiation (encompassing the whole ambit of brand identification, service, capacity for timely delivery and so on that generates reluctance on the part of customers to change supplier) or, more simply, price. In the future this might also need to consider how pervasive Internet use becomes in making differences in some product prices across different sellers more transparent to consumers (see Butler *et al.*, 1997, and Hagel and Armstrong, 1997).

2   The geographic manifestation of competition now and in the future: international, national, or regional competition might have different implications for an industry and its participant companies.

For example, it is sometimes argued that an industry leader may have the financial muscle to take a longer-term view of its prospects and might initiate increased competition in an industry in an attempt to remove weaker and less able competitors, and warn off potential entrants. However, Garda and Marn (1993) draw inferences from example and argue that such a strategy does not always lead to the desired outcome. They make reference to the US airline industry during the period 1990 to 1993 which was characterised by deep competition and price rivalry with heavy losses due to overcapacity. Much of this excess capacity was, however, recycled as new entrants purchased many operators that had collapsed at near forced sale prices. The effect was that these new entrants could operate on a lower than previous cost base.

Consider the creation of Euroland. Although the eleven member nations have taken steps to integrate their economies, at the time of writing taxation regimes vary widely between different member nations. It seems reasonable to hypothesise that tax regimes will need to become increasingly harmonised and trade and labour legislation more standardised if the extent of regional differences in employment, investment and growth are to be reduced. The economics of basic corporate strategy suggest the following.

1   Lower barriers to regional market entry should encourage increased competition and thus convergence of regional price differences for competing goods. However, exactly how relative pricing across regions might become manifest remains to be seen. Empirical evidence on the US market suggests that allowing for regional standards of living and labour productivity gives a different picture from that implied by simple relative price comparisons (see Gompertz, 1997).

2   Best business practice can be expected to transfer across the different member economies as cross-border deregulation and liberalisation increase competitive threats. Lewis *et al.* (1993) argue that foreign direct investment is central to moving innovation around the world. It seems reasonable to hypothesise that a less encumbered movement of capital

between Euroland member nations will only serve to reinforce such a process within the region.

3   Companies that previously held domestic market dominance might increasingly be seen as regionalised in the context of a much larger Euroland and face increased competitive threats from new entrants into their traditional markets. In order to mitigate the potential for an intensification of competitive threats, some companies might attempt to consolidate their industry.

Of course, Euroland is still far removed from many of these potential considerations. Pressures to force change may take many years to manifest themselves or other factors might arise to alter the direction of change indicated by such considerations. However, mergers and acquisitions have recently grown in Euroland although in part this also reflected the global competitive environment at that time.

Integration may involve companies that compete directly with each other (*horizontal integration*). Although all companies are demand-dependent for their well-being (or otherwise), some industries historically have also been characterised by relatively wider swings in their output capacity which have tended to accentuate the effects of changes in industry demand (see, for example, Achi *et al.*, 1996). Some industries that are consolidating face fewer threats from new industry capacity. These industries tend to become more disciplined when constructing new capacity and consolidation means some companies feed their desire for greater scale from the existing industry capacity. Others may attempt to integrate with companies that are in complementary stages of the industry chain (*vertical integration*, for the interested reader; this is discussed in Stuckey and White, 1993). Some companies may integrate even though they are in different industries (*lateral integration*). Some companies integrate indirectly, where a partial stake is held in other companies, but control is effectively in the hands of the partial stakeholder.

The question of accounting

Although financial accounts are *ex post*, they have sometimes been subject to a number of interpretations so that the accounting emphasis might be suited to short-term considerations (we shall refer to this as accounting creativity). Nevertheless, fundamentalists base a large part of their understanding of a company on its accounts. Principal amongst this is an investigation of the *quality* of a company's reported performance, cash flow generation and its asset (book) base. However, companies are manifestly varied and even in the same industry they may face different situations that, in order to provide a true and fair view and profit and loss, might dictate different accounting treatments. Unsurprisingly, most generally accepted accounting practices accommodate this by offering some flexibility to the producers of accounts. While it is understandable that a company may not want to give away too much information about its activities to its buyers, suppliers, or potential and actual competitors, accounting creativity will usually mean that transparency in the accounts is reduced.

Much of the accounting creativity has focused on declaring a desired profit or loss account, balance sheet or cash flow generation. On the face of it, one of the more obvious examples was under the old UK Statement of Standard Accounting Practice 6 (SSAP 6) which made a distinction between exceptional items (used in reported earnings per share) and extraordinary items (not used in reported earnings per share). This meant certain accounting items could be classified as exceptional where they enhanced reported earnings and as extraordinary when they did not. SSAP 6 has since been superseded by a different financial reporting standard and other examples of accounting creativity have meant the accounting standards regulator has continued to tighten up in the more recent standards.

The nature of the business of some companies means they can have exclusion from specified generally accepted accounting practices or can apply particular accounting approaches (for example, statement of recommended practice, or SORP). Some financial companies may fall into this category. Companies whose business is the exploration and production of oil may consciously offer a reconciliation of the historic cost earnings with that of replacement cost earnings that aims to better reflect the underlying performance and help dampen the distortions caused by volatile gains or loses on their inventories. Other companies can have exclusion from specified generally accepted accounting practices. For example, investment companies (as set out in the Companies Act 1985, section 266) have arrangements to treat certain unrealised losses of a capital nature in their accounts differently from other companies.

Sales (turnover) analysis

The profit and loss (P&L) account is one of the primary statements of the performance of a company, the more detailed version usually relating to the situation over a year. A variety of P&L formats occur in practice. A parent company will usually have its own P&L while many larger organisations will also provide consolidated P&L accounts (representing the aggregate results for a parent company and its subsidiary undertakings, although there may be scope for the exclusion of some subsidiaries from consolidation).

Although many companies sell more than one product, economic theory provides a useful framework for investigating properties of these individually in the market place. For a single product, sales (turnover) can then be analysed as the sales volume (number of units sold) multiplied by the sales price per unit. To provide a measure of the responsiveness of supply to another influence, the concept of *elasticity of supply* was developed. The influence may reflect any of the inputs at each stage of a production process, or may relate to goods that go to the final consumer. However, we will, concentrate on the analogous concept associated with consumer demand. Two of the important variables that economists hypothesised as having an effect on the quantity demanded of a good are its price and the degree of substitution.

The sensitivity of the quantity of a good demanded to its price, *ceteris paribus*, can be measured by the *coefficient of price elasticity of demand*. Numerically, the coefficient of price elasticity of quantity demanded for a very small price change is given as:

$$e_X = -\frac{\Delta Q_X}{\delta P_X} \times \frac{P_X}{Q_X}$$

where: e_X = coefficient of price elasticity of quantity demanded of good X;

P_X = price of good X;

δP_X = small change in the price of good X;

Q_X = quantity demanded of good X over a unit of time; and

ΔQ_X = change in the quantity demanded of good X resulting from the change in the price of good X.

Economic theory suggests there is normally an inverse relationship between the price and the quantity of a good demanded in the market place. If e_X is greater than one, the quantity of a good X demanded is said to be *price elastic* and a small percentage change in its price is related to a greater percentage change in its quantity demanded. If e_X is less than one, the quantity of good X demanded is said to be *price inelastic* and the impact of a small price change is related to a less than proportionate change in its quantity demanded. If e_X equals one, the quantity of good X demanded is said to be *unitary price elastic* and a percentage change in its price is related to the same percentage change in its quantity demanded. Price elasticity of demand is often explained by considering two elements.

1   The number and closeness of substitutes. This suggests, *ceteris paribus*, if the price of a good rises, consumers will substitute the good in favour of other goods and so the demand for it will fall; if the price fell, consumers

will substitute other goods in its favour and so the demand for it will rise. In this sense, the relative price (from a change in the goods price) is the major determining factor on the quantity demanded of the good. Most goods have a number of possible substitutes, but the degree of substitution between them is likely to vary.

2   The length of time to which the price change applies (indeed, all factors that affect demand would generally relate to a specified time period).

If the price of a good is plotted on the vertical axis and the quantity demanded is plotted on the horizontal axis, these considerations illustrate why a demand curve will normally slope downwards from left to right. We can, however, make this analysis more complex. *Ceteris paribus,* a change in the price of a good will result in a change in consumers' real income. The resulting effect on the quantity demanded is known as the *income effect.* For example, if the price of a normal good fell, the quantity demanded will usually increase because it has become more affordable. For so-called *inferior goods,* however, the income effect works in an opposite or negative fashion: that is, given a change in the price of a good, the quantity demanded of an inferior good resulting from the income effect changes in the same direction as that price change. Ordinarily, the substitution effect (from a change in the price of the good) is sufficient to offset any negative income effect, but in some cases this may not occur, with the result that the demand for a good moves directionally with its price change (over some range of prices). Goods with this feature are known as 'Giffen goods' although such goods are thought to be extremely rare.

In practice, the demand for a good is affected by a myriad of factors. More generally, the change in the quantity demanded of a good may arise because of a change in relative prices over some time interval (the *substitution effect*). Therefore, rather than a change in the price of the good under investigation, demand may relate to the effect on the good from a change in the price of its substitute goods. Further considerations relate to the availability and willingness of consumers to undertake purchases using debt. Other considerations may relate to a change in consumer tastes and fashions. This latter feature is more important in some industries than others: for example, fashion trends are obviously important in the fashion industry.

Nevertheless, the notion of price elasticity of demand is useful because it highlights the fact that, generally, companies will not only be affected differently by different pricing environments, but also by the same unit degree of pricing pressure according to the price sensitivity of the demand for the goods they sell. Thus, the environment of competitive pressure can also manifest itself in the degree of possible substitution, which will usually vary from industry to industry. The greater the homogeneity of a good with others, the greater the potential substitution effect will tend to be.

However, an absolute (pure) monopoly, which occurs when a single company offers the whole supply of some good, suggests a general absence of, or weakness in, possible substitute goods. In practice, monopoly power is defined in a much broader sense (by, for example, the UK Monopolies and Mergers Commission) so that the structure of market monopoly is often more complex and usually involves more than one company. The time component and affordability as measured by buyers' real incomes may also affect demand. For example, the creation of the Organisation of Petroleum Exporting Countries (OPEC) formed a market for oil that led to a large concentration of pricing power in the cartel's hands. As a result, the cartel had the influence to determine the selling price of oil (although not the volume of oil sold) as happened, for example, in late 1973.

The income and substitution effects are also used in an analogous fashion to argue that, for many industries, the effect on sales is influenced by the aggregate demand in the wider economy. Such an effect is sometimes associated with the notion of credit creation or a similar concept, known as the *multiplier effect*, propounded by John Maynard Keynes (1936). In one of its simpler forms, demand creation is modelled to flow through an economy as a geometric progression. For example, imagine an economy that has surplus capacity in all its productive resources. Suppose a marginal amount of additional investment is undertaken, *ceteris paribus*, so that incomes rise by £100 and, at each subsequent point where money is exchanged, 90 per cent is spent and the recipient of the money saves 10 per cent. The effect is a sequence as shown in Table 4.1.

If the sequence shown in the table carries on for ever, then at the limit, the £100 originally spent creates demand in the economy equivalent to £1000 given by $£100/(1 - MPC)$ where MPC is the economy's marginal propensity to consume. Relaxing the *ceteris paribus* assumption, each transaction is likely to involve variable expenditures on a number of different products, reflecting each consumer's spending preferences. Of course, Keynes's analysis included a number of variables beyond simply the multiplier. Some economic

Table 4.1 *Illustration of the multiplier effect*

Transaction	Amount received (£)	Amount saved (£)	Amount spent (£)
1	100		100
2	100	10	90
3	90	9	81
etc.	...	...	...
etc.	...	...	...
Total			1000

theorists believe the results from his analyses form a special case so that a number of economic theories (either static or dynamic) developed to help explain how economic variables can interrelate to affect aggregate demand and output (see Niemira and Klein, 1994).

Operating multipliers

A number of different formats of the profit and loss account arise in UK practice. Some break down costs according to function, and so provide a cost of sales figure. The difference between sales (turnover) and the cost of sales is the gross profit. The ratio of the gross profit to sales, expressed as a percentage, is the gross profit margin.

The operating profit, or trading profit (in some UK accounts an operating profit is defined after allowing for associates, but we shall exclude associates in this book), is the sales (turnover) less the operating costs. The operating margin (in percentage form) is given by:

$$\text{Operating margin (\%)} = \frac{\text{Operating profit/(loss)}}{\text{Sales}} \times 100$$

This aims to measure profitability independent of company financing structure and tax. Both the gross and operating margins will tend to be both industry and company specific.

Operating multipliers attempt to reflect the degree to which a company's operating profit is sensitive to its sales. Although in practice it is rare to provide an unambiguous classification of costs as being simply variable or fixed, we shall make this simplifying assumption. Let us define:

$$\begin{aligned}
\text{LSV} &= \text{Level of sales volume over a given unit of time} \\
\text{FOC} &= \text{Fixed operating costs associated with the LSV} \\
\text{VCU} &= \text{Variable costs per unit of the LSV} \\
\text{SPU} &= \text{Sales price per unit of the LSV}
\end{aligned}$$

We shall assume, unless stated otherwise, that the company's output is equal to its LSV. For a single product, sales (turnover) equals selling price per unit times sales volume. Assuming a linear relationship between costs and LSV (that is, assuming FOC and VCU are both constant), a small change (indicated by the prefix δ) in SPU or LSV or both simultaneously over a unit period of time offers the following relationships:

$$\Delta\text{Sales} = \delta\text{LSV} \times \text{SPU} + \text{LSV} \times \delta\text{SPU} + \delta\text{LSV} \times \delta\text{SPU}$$

$$\Delta\text{Operating Profit} = \delta\text{LSV} \times (\text{SPU} - \text{VCU}) + \text{LSV} \times \delta\text{SPU}$$
$$+ \delta\text{LSV} \times \delta\text{SPU}$$

where Δ refers to 'a change in' the parameter it prefixes.

These expressions can help to illustrate relationships between sales and operating profit caused by changes in LSV, SPU or both simultaneously under a constant unit cost structure assumption. The latter situation is complex and this analysis is sometimes further simplified by assuming that changes in LSV and SPU are mutually exclusive, allowing the effect on operating profit to be separated into an operational volume multiplier effect and an operational price multiplier effect.

Operational volume multiplier (OVM)

This is sometimes described as *operational gearing* or *operational leverage*. The expressions 'gearing' or 'leverage' used in the context of a company's cost structure reflect the degree of percentage sensitivity to fixed costs (it is useful to separate gearing into financial and operating, although the latter is sometimes used in a combined context to include both forms of gearing). Companies whose operating costs are largely fixed are said to have high operational gearing, and thus a high OVM. Assuming FOC is greater than zero:

Operational volume multiplier (OVM) =

$$\frac{\Delta \text{Operating profit\% (caused by a 1\% change in LSV, } ceteris\ paribus)}{\delta \text{Sales\% (caused by a 1\% change in LSV, } ceteris\ paribus)}$$

The greater the OVM, the greater the tendency for operating profit to vary with respect to the volatility of sales volume. Consider, for example, the companies A and B in Table 4.2. Because both companies have the same LSV and cost structure, operating profit will change by the same amount for a 1 per

Table 4.2 *Example: operational volume multiplier*

	Company A	Company B
LSV	80 000	80 000
FOC	£180 000	£120 000
VCU	£7	£7
SPU	£10	£10
Operating profit	£60 000	£120 000
Actual change in operating profit for a 1% change in LSV, *ceteris paribus*	£2 400	£2 400
OVM	4	2

cent change in LSV: that is, £2400. However, company A is more operationally geared than company B. Thus, for a 1 per cent increase in the volume of sales, company A will show a 4 per cent increase in operating profit, and company B a 2 per cent increase. This might seem fine when sales volumes are rising, but for a 1 per cent fall in the volume of sales, company A will show a fall in operating profit of 4 per cent and company B a 2 per cent fall.

In practice, it is the combination of LSV volatility and the OVM that determines the sales volume risk to operating profit. Thus, it should also be separately related to the potential change in sales volume, since companies with a high OVM might still experience a small change in volume and those with a low OVM might still experience a large change in volume. Further, the assumption that SPU, VCU and FOC remain constant implies a short-term analysis since these are unlikely to remain constant over longer periods.

Operational price multiplier (OPM)

This reflects the percentage change in operating profit for a 1 per cent change in unit-selling price (SPU):

Operational price multiplier (OPM) =

$$\frac{\Delta\,\text{Operating profit\% (caused by a 1\% change in SPU, \textit{ceteris paribus})}}{\delta\,\text{Sales\% (caused by a 1\% change in SPU, \textit{ceteris paribus})}}$$

For example, consider the hypothetical companies A and B in Table 4.3.

Table 4.3 *Example: operational price multiplier*

	Company A	Company B
LSV	90 000	90 000
FOC	£180 000	£90 000
VCU	£7	£7
SPU	£10	£10
Statistics:		
Sales	£900 000	£900 000
Operating profit	£90 000	£180 000
Actual change in operating profit for a 1% change in SPU, *ceteris paribus*	£900	£900
OPM	10	5

As both companies have the same LSV and SPU, the operating profit will change by the same amount for a 1 per cent change in selling price per unit LSV: that is, £900. However, A's operating profit is more price sensitive than B's. For a 1 per cent increase in selling price per unit LSV, company A will show a rise in operating profit of 10 per cent and company B an increase of 5 per cent. The converse will apply for a 1 per cent fall in selling price per unit LSV: that is, company A will show a fall in operating profit of 10 per cent and company B a fall of 5 per cent. More generally, this analysis should also be related separately to the tendency of a company to experience price change since OPM reflects an effect not a cause. The assumption that LSV, VCU and FOC are constant once again implies a short-term analysis.

Maximising operating profit

A comparison of the operational volume multiplier and operational price multiplier over a common unit period of time for a given cost structure and product price assuming VCU > 0 suggests:

Operational Volume Multiplier < Operational Price Multiplier

An illustration is shown in Figure 4.5 that assumes a positive operating profit under a constant cost structure and given SPU at different LSV. However, as already noted, an OVM or OPM will reflect more than simply LSV. For example, an OPM will vary as operating margin varies. Therefore, to relate price and volume sensitivities involves an intricate analysis, but an example is

Figure 4.5   *An example of the OVM and OPM under a constant cost structure and given SPU at different LSV (assuming a positive operating profit)*

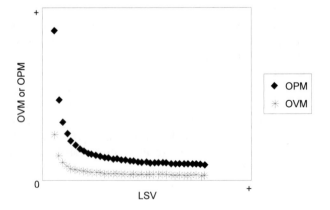

provided by Garda and Marn (1993) who investigated the profit sensitivity to price in respect of an aggregation of the top 1000 companies in the USA using Compustat data. At the time of their study, they determined that if prices fell by a single percentage point and costs and volume remained unchanged, operating profit could be expected to fall by 12.3 per cent. Given the marginal contribution, they deduced that the price elasticity of demand needed to be more than twice that value only rarely exceeded in practice for volume to offset the effect of a one percentage point change in price.

In assessing the potential impact from an OPM or OVM a range of considerations would be required, including a company's potential to experience price change relative to volume change. This might reflect factors outside an industry's control, but in looking at price, Garda and Marn (1993) provide insights into the actual and potential competitive consequences of a change in relative product pricing. Although they argue that initiating price competition can in some situations form part of a company's sound overall strategic programme, they explain, for example, that customers buy in terms of the perceived benefits derived from a product (for instance, quality and technical service or support) less its price. Thus they reason that inappropriate downward pricing initiatives run the risk of a counter-price reaction by competitors so that as this plays out, this can also leave customers with expectations that can become distorted and potentially more sensitive to product price rather than its value and benefits. It might be the case that such action, for example, helps accelerate product demand, but if a premium price is being charged and the company values this, then one risk of a price war is that this premium price becomes eroded.

Business risk and other practical considerations

Since the degree of operational volume gearing is a measure of risk (that is, volatility) to the operating profit, it is often regarded as being an analogue to *business risk*. Business risk (or operating risk) usually refers to the degree to which operating profit is unpredictable or uncertain. A high OVM leads to greater business risk, but business risk also depends on factors other than simply a variation in LSV. Operating profit may also fluctuate because of changes in price, volumes and price simultaneously or total cost (VCU, FOC or both). (In its more general sense, business risk is also a function of the myriad of different business influences that can result in increased operating uncertainty on a company that may be structural or temporary.) In considering the operational gearing to sales (from volumes, prices or both simultaneously), the assumption that VCU and FOC are constant will usually relate to a short-term analysis since costs will be unlikely to remain constant over longer periods and over all ranges of output.

Interest gearing multiplier

Companies have a number of options in raising finance. Bank loans, a bond or new issue of equity, or retaining rather than paying dividends are some of the traditional methods. Debt, for example, normally incurs interest expenses. However, companies normally borrow to invest in sources of revenue from which they also expect an appropriate rate of return.

Finance costs can be either fixed rate or variable rate. Let us assume that these are all fixed. Interest gearing can be defined in a number of ways, but we will generalise it as the percentage sensitivity of profit before tax (PBT) to a small percentage change in operating profit. Let us denote:

Operating profit/ (loss)   = OP
Finance costs (assumed fixed) = FFC

If a 1 per cent change in operating profit (δOP) leads to a change in PBT (ΔPBT) over a short period of time, the interest gearing multiplier (IGM) can then be given as follows:

$$IGM = \frac{\Delta PBT/PBT}{\delta OP/OP}$$

Consider the example in Table 4.4. Company A and company B each incorporate the same operating profit but with different levels of interest costs (assumed fixed). While the change in PBT shows the same actual change for a 1 per cent change in operating profit, they show a very different pattern of percentage change (A: 2 per cent; B: 1 per cent), depending on the interest gearing multiplier. The converse of a 1 per cent fall in operating profit to the sensitivity on PBT will also reflect relative differences in interest costs.

Table 4.4   *An illustration of the interest gearing multiplier*

	Company A £	Company B £
OP	60 000	60 000
Interest payable	(30 000)	0
PBT	30 000	60 000
Statistics		
Actual change in PBT for a 1% rise in operating profit, *ceteris paribus*	600	600
IGM	2	1

Total multiplier

If a high OVM or OPM (or the effect of both price and volume changes simultaneously) is combined with a high interest gearing multiplier, the effect on pre-tax earnings growth can be dramatic. A total multiplier is a measure of the multiple of profit effect associated with the combined effects of the operational multipliers (from sales volumes, prices or both simultaneously) and an interest gearing multiplier.

Assuming a VCU, FOC and FFC are constant, then if a δSales% (from volumes, prices or both simultaneously) leads to a ΔOP% that leads to a ΔPBT%, the total multiplier (TM) can be represented by:

$$
\begin{aligned}
\text{TM} &= \text{Operational multiplier (from volume, price or both} \\
&\quad \text{simultaneously, } \textit{ceteris paribus}) \times \text{Interest Gearing Multiplier} \\
&= \frac{\Delta\text{OP}\%}{\delta\text{Sales}} \times \frac{\Delta\text{PBT}\%}{\Delta\text{OP}\%} \\
&= \frac{\Delta\text{PBT}\%}{\delta\text{Sales}\%}
\end{aligned}
$$

The rate of change in earnings per share growth (over a continuous time horizon or from period to period) is one of the many definitions of what is called *earnings momentum*. Earnings momentum may be described as rising (positive) or falling (negative). Allowing for the impact of tax and other appropriations separately, earnings momentum can become related to the total multiplier (assuming no share issue). In practice, the changing mix of volume and price in sales may adjust rapidly and the operating and financial structure of a company will vary over time. As a result, the primary limitation of a total multiplier lies in the assumptions that VCU, FOC and FFC are constant across all ranges of output and time frames.

Break-even analysis

Break-even analysis seeks to assess the interrelationship between a company's output and its total costs at the point where profits are zero: that is, at the break-even point. Break-even analysis examines the effects of small changes in sales volume on before or after tax profit. An example of a linear relationship between costs and sales volume is illustrated in Figure 4.6. From this graph, as the level of sales volume increases, so does the cost of manufacturing the new level of output. Below the break-even point, the company is unable to recover its total costs given selling price per unit, with the result that a loss is incurred. Above the break-even point, total costs are

Figure 4.6 *Break-even volume of sales under a linear relationship between costs and sales volume*

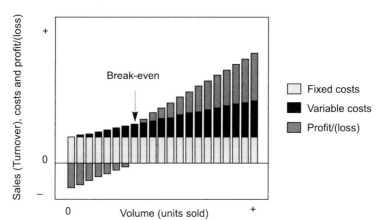

recovered at a given selling price per unit, and the company starts to earn a profit.

For a company making a single product let us continue with the assumption of a linear relationship between costs and output. At the break-even point, there is no pre-tax profit so there is assumed to be no tax (we ignore the practical implications of tax timing differences), and the company is said to break even. The break-even level of sales volume (LSV_{be}) can then be ascertained or, given LSV, the break-even sales price per unit (SPU_{be}) can be given as the sum of the total fixed costs per unit of LSV plus the variable costs per unit of LSV.

Consider the example in Table 4.5. Given this total cost structure, break-even sales point occurs at 50 000 units under A, and zero units under B (since this company makes a loss at all levels of positive sales), and 25 000 units under C. Equally, the break-even price is seen to fall as the total costs fall, illustrated by comparing A and C; under B, the SPU of £9 results in a loss at all levels of output, and an SPU_{be} of £11 is needed to break even at a sales volume of 100 000 units.

Including production overheads in the cost of finished goods in manufacturing when valuing stocks means these will not simply be classified as fixed or variable as assumed in the above break-even analysis. Since, in a perfect market, the market decides whether a company can sell either the LSV_{be} at the assumed SPU or the LSV at the SPU_{be}, budgeting the level of production forms an important management decision. For example, overproduction

Table 4.5 *An example of break-even values*

	A	B	C
LSV	£100 000	£100 000	£100 000
FOC + FFC	£100 000	£100 000	£50 000
VCU	£10.00	£10.00	£10.00
SPU	£12.00	£9.00	£12.00
LSV_{be}	50 000	0	25 000
SPU_{be}	£11.00	£11.00	£10.50

relative to sales (turnover) reduces the unit fixed production costs absorbed by LSV. The effect might potentially be to produce enhanced declared profits without a necessary improvement in the demand outlook on the company (albeit that the additional investment in unsold stock will need to be financed). Moreover, an analyst would need to use judgement in assessing whether any extra stock units will be met by eventual rising sales (turnover). This analysis becomes even more complicated in situations where a company has more than one product. Further, in practice, costs will not increase linearly with sales (over all ranges of output or over all time frames) as we have assumed. For example, capacity constraints might lead to expenditure on additional plant and machinery that cause a variation in fixed costs, and input costs might vary according to the discount received on quantity ordered. Further, not all finance costs are likely to be fixed but, even where these were originally fixed, they could be varied by financial engineering or could be refinanced at different rates of interest. Thus linearity may not always be a practical assumption, in which event there may be more than one break-even point at different LSVs.

Remodelling the typical business model

The typical business model is based on income and costs, assets and liabilities and cash flow. The notion of income and costs is probably the easiest to understand. Assets and liabilities are formed in the balance sheet which makes a distinction between the long-term assets of a business, called fixed assets, and the short-term assets, called current assets. Fixed assets are usually depreciated, although sometimes certain fixed assets might also be stated at some revaluation. Although insolvency may involve a situation where the winding-up of a business would realise insufficient assets to repay all liabilities in full, the values in the balance sheet do not purport to reflect either the potential winding-up value or the potential going concern value of a business.

The link between income, costs and the balance sheet items is usually based on ratio analysis. Whilst there are many possible accounting ratios, each will aim to offer insights into particular aspects of a business. For example, return on capital employed (ROCE) can be defined simply as:

ROCE = Operating profit/Capital employed

In practice, a company's ROCE has been defined in various ways, and there are numerous accounting considerations in determining an appropriate measure of capital employed. An analyst might therefore adjust the values taken directly from the annual report and accounts to determine a more appropriate measure of operating profit or capital employed and to make these more consistent with each other.

ROCE attempts to measure the effectiveness of sales and efficiency independently of balance sheet structure and tax. For example, the following is a two ratio breakdown:

ROCE = Operating profit/Turnover × Turnover/Capital employed

= Operating margin × Capital employed turnover

Thus a company may increase its ROCE by improving its operating margin or increasing its capital employed turnover. The former will be influenced by a company's price and volume mix of sales (turnover) and costs. The capital employed turnover is a measure of a company's effectiveness at employing its capital, since it indicates the number of times capital employed is turned over in a year. The greater this number, the lower the capital employed over the given range of sales (turnover) that was required for a company to generate a unit level of sales (turnover).

One of the limitations of many financial ratios is that they fail to consider the cash generation of a business. The importance of cash flow is rarely overemphasised. Ultimately, a business is run with cash: to pay wages/ salaries, cost of materials for manufacture, rent and rates, interest on loans, taxes and dividends. Different companies (even in the same industry) may exhibit different levels of cash generation. While accounting-based ratios can offer useful insights, relating these to the level of cash generation aims to highlight whether a company is able, ultimately, to self-finance future expectations and is using its cash flow in a way that adds (rather than destroys) value for its shareholders. Analysts use a number of proxies for cash flow, but this does not remove a need to consider its source, its security and the firm's ease of access to it.

The impact of technology on telecommunications and the Internet on how businesses channel their sales is still in its infancy, but it is argued that these developments offer a number of opportunities and potential emerging threats (see Harrington and Reed, 1996). Implied by these developments is that, ultimately, there might be a need for some existing business models to be remodelled. In general, consider the following examples of the potential impact from the consumer.

1   Ordering of goods via the Internet is done through the press of a button. Assuming enough goods are sold through the medium of the Internet, it is possible to hypothesise that the geographic market proximity of stock (inventory) to consumers for many products will become less of an issue. If so, this offers the prospect of less duplication across regions, and ratios such as stock (inventory) to sales for many companies might need to be remodelled.

2   If Internet technology develops and becomes more widespread, regional product pricing information is likely to become more transparent. As a result, use of the Internet will form a more efficient cross-regional market pricing intermediary for some goods. The eventual impact will, however, depend upon the strength of supplier-created barriers, although some countries are already trying to bring down such impediments to market efficiency. If so, profit margins derived from a market that obscures regional price differences for comparable product offerings might need to be remodelled. Even if regional product pricing is not an issue, increased competition from the Internet for comparable product offerings might still have competitive implications for today's typical business model. For example, Bowers and Singer (1996) looked at the competitive development and the likely future implications for coming market operators in the US on-line personal financial services industry. While they confess to the impossibility of predicting the eventual economics, they conclude that much of the value derived from computer-based banking will probably be transferred to the consumer in the form of lower prices and new value-added information and service offerings.

The implication of the Internet's effect on the typical business model has yet to make its full mark on many of them. Discussion with a number of analysts appears to draw a mixed response on the extent of the Internet's expected ultimate effect from the consumer on the typical business model. Possible inferences might be drawn from anticipated trends in advertising, but based on interviews with marketing executives, Cartellieri et al. (1997) found that many believed that the impact of the Internet would not change their approach to advertising. Of course, guessing the future based on the current stage of Internet development is subject to a high degree of uncertainty, but Cartellieri et al. (1997) took a different view.

References and further reading

Achi, Z., J. Hausen, A. Nick, J. L. Pfeffer, and P. Verhaeghe (1996) 'Managing capacity in basic materials', *The McKinsey Quarterly*, no. 1, pp. 58–65.

Bowers, T. and M. Singer (1996), 'Who will capture value in on-line financial services?', *The McKinsey Quarterly*, no. 2, pp. 78–83.

Bughin, J. and T. E. Copeland (1997) 'The virtuous circle of shareholder value creation', *The McKinsey Quarterly*, no. 2, pp. 157–67.

Butler, P., T. W. Hall, A. M. Hanna, L. Mendonca, B. August, J. Manyika and A. Sahay (1997) 'A revolution in interaction', *The McKinsey Quarterly*, no. 1, pp. 4–23.

Cartellieri, C., A. J. Parsons, V. Rao and M. P. Zeisser (1997) 'The real impact of Internet advertising', *The McKinsey Quarterly*, no. 3, pp. 44–62.

Copeland, T. E. (1994) 'Why value value?', *The McKinsey Quarterly*, no. 4, pp. 97–109.

Copeland, T., T. Koller and J. Murrin (1996) *Valuation – Measuring and Managing the Value of Companies*, 2nd edn (New York: John Wiley).

Garda, R. A. and M. V. Marn (1993) 'Price wars', *The McKinsey Quarterly*, no. 3, pp. 87–100.

Glucksman, M. and J. Morecroft (1998) 'Managing metamorphosis', *The McKinsey Quarterly*, no. 2, pp. 118–29.

Gompertz, A. (1997) 'Current research: Price level adjustments challenge assumptions about regional standards of living', *The McKinsey Quarterly*, no. 1, pp. 185–9.

Hagel III, J. and A. G. Armstrong (1997) 'Net gain: Expanding markets through virtual communities', *The McKinsey Quarterly*, no. 2, pp. 140–53.

Harrington, L. and G. Reed (1996) 'Electronic commerce (finally) comes of age', *The McKinsey Quarterly*, no. 2, pp. 68–77.

Keynes, J. M. (1936) *The General Theory of Employment, Interest, and Money* (New York: Harcourt Brace & Co.).

Lewis, W. W., H. Gersbach, T. Jansen and K. Sakate (1993) 'The secret to competitiveness – competition', *The McKinsey Quarterly*, no. 4, pp. 29–43.

Nevens, T. M, J. R. Guiniven and A. B. Paulsen (1998) 'The key to success in electronics: Shifting the balance between profit and growth', *The McKinsey Quarterly*, no. 2, pp. 140–7.

Niemira, M. P. and P. A. Klein (1994) *Forecasting Financial and Economic Cycles*, (New York: John Wiley).

Porter, M. E. (1980) *Competitive Strategy* (New York: The Free Press).

Stuckey, J. and D. White (1993), 'When and when *not* to vertically integrate', *The McKinsey Quarterly*, no. 3, pp. 3–27.

5   Equity Valuation Analysis

Introduction

As the present value of the sum of a future cash flow stream, the discounted cash flow methodology of investment value is not a complex notion. Some professional equity analysts use this notion in various ways and with various levels of sophistication in an attempt to assess the attractiveness of a share given its current market price. However, a number of other situations might influence the market price because the stock market investor operates in a dynamic environment where the valuation emphasis can vary. For example, there are companies that invest in underlying assets for which an expected change in the underlying capital value of the assets might form a stronger motive force to share ownership. Recognition of this aspect often leads to one example of an asset value approach to equity valuation. Depending upon the scarcity and outlook of those underlying assets or their probability of being realised, the equity market value will be at parity, or at a premium, or at a discount to the value of the underlying assets.

Price-to-accounting theories

A number of more common valuation approaches have been proffered. Each can be recast in terms of a DCF type arrangement, but they apply simplifying assumptions to make the notion of value less onerous. Examples include the price-to-earnings ratio model; sales-to-equity market capitalisation model; price-to-dividend ratio model; and market-to-book ratio model.

Price-to-earnings (P/E) ratio

Generally, this approach is usually thought to have less applicability to emerging growth companies, although it is still one of the more ubiquitous ratios. It is given as:

P/E ratio = Market price per share/EPS

where EPS = (positive) earnings per share (see Figure 5.1). It is common to determine a past rolling P/E multiple using some measure of (normalised) EPS (not to be confused with economic cycle adjusted earnings, sometimes

Figure 5.1   *UK equity market P/E ratio*

Source: Primark Datastream, reproduced with permission.

referred to as normalised earnings) generated over a company's last trading year (or the previous 12–month rolling trading period). However, if the future EPS is forecast correctly, then it will eventually become the historic EPS. The *prospective P/E* ratio relates the forecast EPS to the current market share price. The greater the P/E ratio, the greater the rating or earnings multiple is said to be. P/E ratio analysis is applied both as an absolute and as a relative earnings-based measure of valuation. Many analysts generate their forecast earnings based on fundamental analysis and estimate a price for earnings to the end of an expected holding period from industry or market analysis (for a review of a number of empirical studies on earnings and the P/E ratio, see Lofthouse, 1994, Chs. 7, 9, 10).

While P/E ratio analysis will usually form a consideration in situations where an appropriate measure of EPS is the market's motive force to share ownership, a company can have a high or low prospective P/E ratio for many reasons. Further P/E multiples are applied in a variety of ways. For example, one simple investment approach is based on standardising a price–earnings ratio by the long-run earnings per share growth rate. Some investors refine this approach by also looking at other potential considerations (for example, earnings momentum).

Sales-to-equity market capitalisation

Some valuation measures relate the value of a company's equity trading in the market to some measure of earnings, cash flow or assets. Moving down a profit and loss account, the number of accounting entries increases and this adds to the difficulties of determining their quality. Because sales (turnover) is the first entry in the profit and loss account, some contend that it is sometimes easier to entertain certain insights into valuation arguments (for a review of a number of empirical studies on a reciprocal sales-to-price strategy, see Lofthouse, 1994).

At the individual stock level, UK analysts appear to discuss the notion of sales as a valuation measure in more specialised situations. In part, this is understandable because although a sales based valuation metric can have implicit relationships to a price-to-earnings and some other share valuation metrics, the relationship can intuitively become somewhat complex. Further, reported sales might not be comparable to alternative industry entities, thus still making within- and across-industry comparisons difficult.

A simple sales-to-equity market capitalisation (S/MC) ratio is represented by:

$$\text{S/MC} = \text{Sales/Equity market capitalisation}$$

The S/MC ratio gives the number of times the equity market capitalisation is covered by the sales (turnover). In other words, it measures the sales per unit of equity market capitalisation. For example, if this ratio were 2, the market would be saying that the company is worth 50p for each £1 of sales. As a model, a sales/equity market capitalisation ratio can be represented in terms of a ratio of sales (per share) to share price (under an unchanged share issue) and thus both a net profit margin and P/E ratio. In practice, the application of a net profit margin and P/E ratio to the model does complicate the relationship although equally it offers greater insights. Further, some analysts adjust the equity market capitalisation to allow for net cash or net debt. In terms of the sales of the firm in relation to the market value of its equity, an analyst might view net cash or net debt as being valued at their cash amounts when making this adjustment. However, companies use cash in a variety of ways and in some cases the stock market might incorporate the probability of an opportunity to use that cash. This latter situation might lead to a scenario-based analysis to model the possibilities.

Consider a hypothetical example of an infant industry comprising twenty operators standing on a price/sales ratio (p/s, the reciprocal of a sales/price ratio) of 30 times while the market overall is on 2. It is then possible to determine the required rate of sales growth for the industry to reach the overall market average p/s at unchanged industry and overall equity market capitalisation. If overall market sales grow at 5% per annum, the industry needs to grow at an average relative rate roughly sixteen times to match the p/s of the market to the end of the fifth year and roughly five times to the end of fifteenth year. By the end of the twentieth year, the required industry sales growth rate falls to roughly four times, and roughly three times to the end of

Figure 5.2 *Example of an industry p/s as the number of industry operators declines assuming a uniform market capitalisation across all those companies at an unchanged level of industry sales (turnover)*

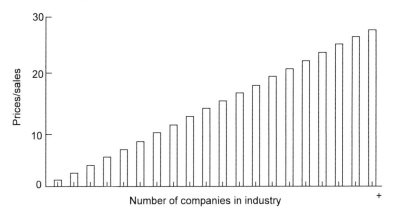

the thirtieth year. These relative rates of growth might differ if one is looking at the relative earnings, cash flow or assets of the industry rather than sales.

If an industry evolves according to the life cycle hypothesis, then the industry dynamics can be expected to change over time so that, for example, it may reach an industry structure that cannot support the same number of companies. As an illustration, let us also assume that the above hypothetical industry is comprised of 20 participants with a uniform market capitalisation across each of these participants. At an unchanged level of industry sales, if the number of industry participants falls to 19, the average (and median) p/s becomes 28.5, falling uniformly to 1.5 times when one participant is left in the industry. This is illustrated in Figure 5.2. To get to a p/s of the market implies less than two companies must remain under the assumption of current industry sales. If we assume the growth in sales of the overall market is 5 per cent p.a., then the required industry growth rate to equal that of the overall market p/s at any given date declines at an increasing rate as the industry mortality rate increases. For example, at the end of ten years, the required growth roughly equals 37 per cent p.a. if 19 companies survive, and decreases to roughly 28 per cent if ten companies survive and 2 per cent if one survives.

Price to dividends (P/DIV)

This takes the share price and divides it by the dividend per share (for a review of a number of empirical studies, see Lofthouse, 1994, and Fama, 1991). Graphically, this is illustrated in Figure 5.3.

Figure 5.3   *UK equity market P/DIV*

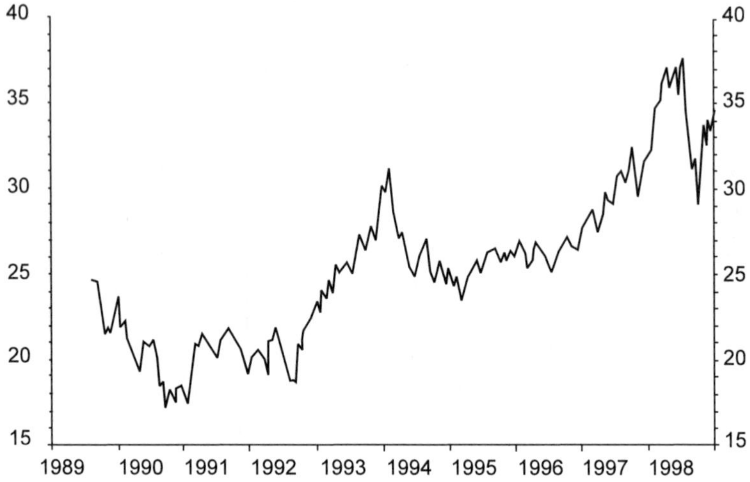

Source: Primark Datastream, reproduced with permission.

Empirically, dividend yields have been found to incorporate information about potential stock market volatility (for example, see Anderson and Breedon, 1996). Some fund managers use the equity market P/DIV as a simple measure of equity modified duration (this term is used interchangeably with duration here since the two are proportional or identical when calculated at the force of interest). For example, with constant dividend payments occurring continuously forever, the resulting cash flow profile will resemble that from a continuously payable fixed income perpetual bond and the duration of such a cash flow stream can be viewed as being equivalent to P/DIV. A variant to the continuous form is the discrete version of the constant-growth dividend discount model (see later). A second, more complex measure allows for dividend growth variations. By varying the growth rate of dividends, the mathematical intricacies rise.

A third measure is given by Leibowitz *et al.* (1989) who suggest that a change in earnings (dividend) growth rate and a change in the dividend discount model's capitalisation rate might not be independent of each other or of other common influences. They make a distinction between a stock's sensitivity with respect to the capitalisation rate, and its interest rate sensitivity as modelled by their formulation. They make the assumption that interest rates reflect an inflation expectation and real component with influence on the capitalisation rate and earnings (and dividend) growth rate. Thus, their formulation stresses relations between stock price changes derived from changes in the inflation and real interest rate components in the capitalisation rate. They also incorporate variables that aim to model the potential change in the equity risk-premium from the same two influences simultaneously. Their formulation thus aims to widen the potential sensitivity dynamics of stock prices according to each change in the assumed components of the capitalisation rate (see also Bernstein, 1995, Ch. 7).

Market-to-book

The ratio of market capitalisation divided by the book value of equity or net worth (the Americanism being used instead of net asset value because the latter is sometimes used ambiguously in the UK) is broadly referred to as market-to-book (or generally price-to-book on a per share basis). For many capital-intensive companies, fixed assets would tend to form a large part of total assets that might also be booked at historic cost. However, accounting policy may invoke the provision for certain fixed assets to be accounted for at some revaluation.

A lower book value of equity for a given level of earnings generates a higher than otherwise return on book equity; a higher book value of equity for a given level of earnings generates a lower than otherwise return on book equity. Thus, the book value support argument needs to be seen in the context of a number of accounting assumptions when, for example, the book value of assets can still be written down (see, for example, Bernstein, 1995, Ch. 2). When trying to calculate a net worth, some analysts might therefore adjust the declared book value to make the accounting treatment of balance sheet items consistent with that of a proposed peer group comparative.

In some situations, book values might not sufficiently distinguish between companies from the same industry (even after allowing for differences in accounting policy). Many insurance companies, for example, write a mixture of life and non-life business, but life assurance is generally seen as a long-term arrangement. As a result, it potentially offers a life office additional long-term profitability (and thus additional potential profitability for its shareholders). An attempt to measure this led to the actuarial notion of *embedded value* which aims to help recognise the future additional value that might be generated from a life office's written book of life business. Thus, measures of market-to-book (or price-to-book) will reflect differences in embedded value when these are incorporated in the value argument.

What is the empirical evidence on market-to-book ratios? This is quite extensive (see, for example, the reviews in Lofthouse, 1994), but here we shall look at the empirical findings of Bryan, Lyons and Rosenthal (1998) who investigated the 100 global companies whose market capitalisation had increased the most between 1992 and 1997. The investigated sample had a base country distribution as follows:

	USA	Canada	European	Asia (mostly Japan)
By headquarters	58	1	30	11

The across-company distribution of these 100 companies is shown in Table 5.1.

On aggregate, they found that these companies grew at a compound annual rate some 1.7 times that of the market average for all large stocks worldwide, while their market-to-book ratios increased from 2.1 in 1992 to 4.2 in 1997. In 1997, they state that the US average market-to-book was about 2. The increase in earnings for the collective group was a compound rate of 23 per cent during the study period, while their return on book equity increased from about 11 per cent to 19 per cent.

To understand the increase in market capitalisation, they divided the growth in market capitalisation into two components: increases in book value and increase in market value over book (the latter forming the primary explanation for the increase in market capitalisation). They then divided these companies into quartiles according to their market-to-book standing in 1997. The results were as follows:

	Quartile 1	Quartile 2	Quartile 3	Quartile 4
Market-to-book ratio	10.7	5.6	3.2	1.9

Although the growth variations in market-to-book between the quartiles were high, the highest grew at about the same rate relative to that of the lowest

Table 5.1 *Across company distribution of the 100 global companies with top performing stocks (1992–7)*

	No. of companies
Largely globalised industries (e.g., petroleum and automotive)	32
Electronics industries (e.g., computers and software)	16
Rapidly globalising industries (e.g., consumer packaged goods and pharmaceuticals)	31
Global companies operating mainly in local industries (e.g., food, insurance and banking)	21
Total	100

quartile. Differences between the quartiles in terms of compound growth in market capitalisation were small (the highest quartile was 26 per cent and the lowest was 20 per cent). The growth in earnings of the highest quartile, at 18 per cent, was found to be less than the lowest quartile at 38 per cent (the lowest quartile being comprised of many turnaround situations). The highest market-to-book quartile had a 1997 return on book equity that was three times that of the lowest quartile, but all four quartiles grew their return on equity by about the same amount over the study period. They reason that differences in the market-to-book ratios reflected closer differences to return on book equity over the study period.

Dividend discount model

Many investors focus on the prospects for a change in a share's market price. For example, consider two similar companies, A and B, operating in the same industry. Let us make the simplifying assumption that both pay annual dividends on the same date with the prospective one year dividend of 4 per cent for company A and 2 per cent for company B. An example of this scenario is set out in Table 5.2. The share price of company A is assumed to have appreciated by 20 per cent and that for company B by 22 per cent at the end of the year. This is not, however, the total one-year rate of return an investor would expect to receive. Consider the dividend income. The expected rate of return at the end of year 1 is then:

	Company A	*Company B*
Share price appreciation	20%	22%
Prospective dividend yield	4%	2%
One-year total expected return	24%	24%

Note: Figures rounded.

The total one-year expected rate of return can be seen to be equal.

Table 5.2 *Example of the forecast share prices of two companies, A and B*

	Company A		*Company B*	
End year:	0	1	0	1
Share Price (growth)	105.0	126 20%	200.0	244.0 22%

Note: All figures rounded.

One model of price behaviour that relies on the relationship to dividends is the dividend discount model. Under the dividend discount model, the dividends are capitalised. The approach therefore discounts dividends to the present time at an appropriate *equity capitalisation rate*. To forecast dividends or the capitalisation rate, a stochastic approach might be taken. Alternative formulations make a discrete interest rate assumption associated with discrete forecasts of the future dividends. The simple dividend discount model assumes both a constant capitalisation rate and that dividends grow at a sustainable constant future long-run rate. In its most basic form, the long term is forever. The present value of annual pay dividends (assuming an equal number of days in each year) where the next dividend is due in one year's time, D_1, under the held forever assumption can be represented as:

$$\text{Present value of dividends} = \frac{D_1}{i - g}$$

where i is the constant dividend capitalisation rate and g the constant growth assumption.

Dividends can be linked to earnings through a payout ratio. Therefore, as a model of equilibrium, it can also be seen in terms of the following parameters: a capitalisation rate, a payout ratio, that rate of return on investments and that proportion of future total earnings financed externally. For example, assume that $i > g$ with investment financed solely from retained earnings and a constant payout ratio. The model then argues that it is not necessary for the capitalisation rate to fall for the growth rate in the present value of the total equity of the firm to exceed the growth rate in total firm earnings. This can be seen in terms of an increase in that rate of return on a firm's investments (a relevant factor in the study by Bryan, Lyons and Rosenthal, 1998).

To help see the extent of growth in value, consider he alternative version of the model. As an illustration, imagine a hypothetical company with the following statistics:

Capitalisation rate	Prospective one year EPS	Growth rate
10.0%	20p	0.0%

The present value is 200p. However, suppose this company can reinvest half its earnings to offer a sustainable rate of growth on that reinvestment of 15 per cent p.a. without changing the risk to the business. At the end of year one, the company retains 10p for investment and pays 10p in dividends.

The investment of 10p produces a return of 15 per cent at the end of year two, (that is, 1.5p). The present value at the end of year one from this constant annual earnings flow forever is 15p and the net present value is $15 - 10 = 5\text{p}$. At the end of year two, the net present value is 7.5 per cent higher than the year before and so on, growing at 7.5 per cent per annum. Therefore, the present value of this stream of net present values is 200p. The sum of the present value of the no-growth assumption and the growth assumption gives a total present value of 400p and the extent of growth in value goes from zero per cent to 50 per cent.

Bruckner *et al.* (1999) elaborate on this notion. To help corporate management draw inferences from their company's market price, they suggest that the total present value might be broken down into a number of time periods: current performance and expected growth prospects. The expected growth prospects are then sub-divided into a short- and long-term element. They take the short term as usually representing two to five years based on market consensus forecasts that are treated as reliable. The difference between current performance and the realised short-term performance when it meets consensus short-term expectations reflects the value expected from short-term growth. The remaining difference between the short-term value of the company and its equity market value represents the anticipated long-term growth. They applied this approach to a number of US industries (pharmaceuticals, networking, publishing, software, multi-business, retail and utilities). Their study showed stock market value was largely reflecting expectations of long-term performance.

The basic dividend discount model is based on a constant growth assumption. However, consistent compound growth above that of the overall market clearly cannot be sustained indefinitely. Other versions of the dividend discount model forecast a specific path for growth. For example, in terms of a short time scale, dividend growth might vary over the peaks and troughs of an economic cycle. Other approaches include normalising earnings over an economic cycle or the theory surrounding the product (industry) life cycle that might involve various stages in a company's development, such as the following:

- growth;
- maturity;
- decline.

As a result, a number of variations in the constant growth dividend discount model have been developed (see, for example the three phase growth model discussed in Fuller, 1979).

A CAPM framework for individual securities

As a risk measure, Markowitz (1959) looked at the statistical measure of standard deviation (and its relation, the variance). Consider, for example, two securities, X and Y, with expected returns and standard deviations as follows:

	X	*Y*
Expected return	18.5%	18.5%
Standard deviation	8.1%	3.5%

Since the expected return has less variation with security Y, it is deemed to have a greater degree of certainty. In other words, investors are assumed to seek the lowest risk measure for a given expected return and are said to be risk-averse (investors are also assumed expected return maximisers so that for a given risk measure, they would seek the greatest expected return). Under the total risk theory, risk is the total standard deviation of security returns. However, whilst equity analysts look at a number of risk factors in the context of an individual security, they often measure potential returns relative to some benchmark, such as the company's peer group or the equity market as a whole. It is therefore significant to investigate how securities might be related to each other.

Diversification deals with the interrelationship of returns between individual securities held as a portfolio (see Markowitz, 1959). To see this, consider two securities viewed as random variables (this is a simplification since a well-diversified portfolio requires more than two securities, for example, see Statman (1987) in respect of stocks). Statistically, the expected return on a linear combination of security X and security Y, $E(R_{wX+(1-w)Y})$, is:

$$E(R_{wX+(1-w)Y}) = w \times E(R_X) + (1-w)(R_Y)$$

where $E(\ldots)$ is the expectations operator and $E(R_X)$ and $E(R_Y)$ the expected return on security X and security Y respectively over the holding period and w is the proportion of funds invested in security X and $1 - w$ the proportion of funds invested in security Y. The return variance of the portfolio is:

$$\sigma^2_{wX+(1-w)Y} = w^2\sigma^2_X + (1-w)^2\sigma^2_Y + 2w(1-w)\sigma_{XY}$$

where $\sigma_{XY} = \rho_{XY}\sigma_X\sigma_Y$ is the return covariance. The expression ρ_{XY} is the return correlation coefficient and is a standardised statistical measure that lies in the range $-1 \leq \rho_{XY} \leq 1$. A weighted average of the individual return standard deviations is given by:

$$w\sigma_X + (1-w)\sigma_Y$$

Therefore, for the portfolio standard deviation to be less than the weighted average of the individual standard deviations, we require:

$$[w^2\sigma_X^2 + (1-w)^2\sigma_Y^2 + 2w(1-w)\sigma_{XY}]^{0.5} < w\sigma_X + (1-w)\sigma_Y$$

which reduces to $\rho_{XY} < 1$. It is therefore possible to combine two securities in such a way as to reduce the relative standard deviation when compared to a weighted average of the individual standard deviations. There are, of course, many ways that securities could be combined, equally weighted or varied in some other way. Consider the previous example again of a security X and security Y with the following statistics:

	X	Y
Expected return	18.5%	18.5%
Standard deviation	8.1%	3.5%

Because the expected returns are the same, the expected return on a linear combination of X and Y will be independent of the portfolio weight w. Mathematically, however, it is possible to find the value of the weight that minimises the portfolio variances, $\sigma^2_{wX+(1-w)Y}$, at any assumed value of ρ_{XY}. An efficient portfolio is defined by having the lowest variance at every associated expected return or the highest expected return at every associated variance.

In practice, the value of ρ_{XY} might be estimated from historic data, r_{XY}, and one of the main considerations with this type of analysis is that the historic value r_{XY} does not necessarily determine the degree of future diversification. The future value of r_{XY} over the expected holding period is a more important indicator of any future diversification.

Based on the notion of diversification is the equilibrium asset pricing theory known as the CAPM. Although there are a number of versions of the CAPM, we will purposely keep the presentation brief and simple in what follows. The CAPM assumes that all investors are efficient portfolio seekers based on expected return and standard deviation derived from identical views about expected return, standard deviation and covariance of individual asset parameters over a common single holding period. Information comes unencumbered and is instantaneously available to all. Restrictions on asset trading do not exist and asset trading occurs without impediment so there are no transaction expenses or taxes and with all assets capable of being bought or sold in any size or amount. All investors are allowed to borrow or lend at a common theoretical risk-free rate of interest that has a known return over the single holding period with the aim of enhancing their end period expected utility.

Since diversification can reduce security risk (standard deviation), implied is that a security can be expected to provide a return commensurate with that part of total risk that cannot be diversified (*systematic risk*). Therefore, because the CAPM is concerned with a sub-set of total security risk, it does not have implications when holding an individual security since this would be concerned with total risk. It can, however, offer theoretical insights into the equilibrium argument for an individual security in the context of adding that security to an efficient portfolio. This is reflected in a theoretical equation known as the security market line (SML: for a quantitative derivation, see, for example, Adams *et al.*, 1993):

Security *s* expected return = Risk-free rate

+ market risk premium × Beta$_s$

The market risk premium is the expected return from the market portfolio less that of the risk-free rate. The beta of security *s* (denoted above by Beta$_s$) represents the covariance of expected returns between security *s* and that on the market portfolio divided by the standard deviation of the expected return on the market portfolio.

The CAPM assumes that individual securities can be seen in the context of an efficient portfolio. Hence it defines the importance of a stock's systematic risk with an exected return related to the expected return on the market portfolio through a beta. The market portfolio should theoretically be comprised of constituents from every possible asset class, where each is market value weighted. However, it is common to view the market portfolio as simply that on ordinary shares (for a critique of this assumption, see Roll, 1977). Further, the market portfolio of equities should comprise all those that are available, but in practice a proxy is used (such as an index).

If the SML is recast as the expected return from a security less that of the risk-free rate, then two measures of the graph are significant in the context of the CAPM (see Figure 5.4).

1   *Alpha.* This is the crossover point of the graph with the security expected return less the risk-free rate axis. Empirically, alpha might be positive, negative or zero, but equilibrium under the CAPM assumptions requires alpha to be zero, since arbitrage in a CAPM market of homogeneous expectations and reaction functions will dictate that no individual alpha would be either positive or negative. Since alpha is the constant of a linear function, empirically two securities with different alphas but equal betas suggest higher returns from the higher alpha security. Some researchers claim to have highlighted certain anomalies such as 'calendar effects' (reviewed in Fama, 1991; Lofthouse, 1993, Ch. 17) where, in general, returns have tended to reflect a calendar pattern. Under a CAPM frame-work, calendar anomalies might be viewed as tactical alpha inefficiencies.

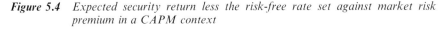

Figure 5.4 *Expected security return less the risk-free rate set against market risk premium in a CAPM context*

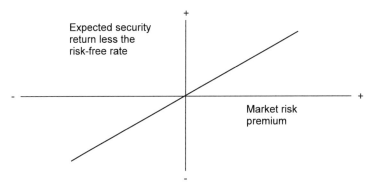

2 *Beta.* This is measured by the gradient of the graph. The effect of the CAPM assumptions is that a security's expected returns less the risk-free rate are proportional to the market risk-premium measured according to its beta.

The SML gives a theoretical justification for the importance of a security's beta. However, tests of the CAPM will usually be concerned with historical data while the model is framed in terms of expectations. Whether the future mirrors the past is a question that can only be answered *ex post*. Statistically, a simpler alternative is the characteristic line (also known as the market model: see Sharpe, 1963) that links security returns directly to the chosen index. This simplification removes a consideration of the covariance relationship between security returns held as a portfolio. The characteristic line will often be based on historical data from some time series regression analysis. Data points that deviate from the line of best fit to the data (the characteristic line) represent a security's returns from effects that would fall outside the market effects captured in the characteristic line.

References and further reading

Adams, A., D. Bloomfield, P. Booth and P. England (1993) *Investment Mathematics and Statistics* (London/Dordrecht/Boston: Graham & Trotman (Kluwer Academic Publishers Group)).
Anderson, N. and F. Breedon (1996) *UK Asset Price Volatility Over the Last 50 Years*, Bank of England Working Paper Series No. 51 (June) (London: Bank of England).
Bernstein, R. (1995) *Style Investing* (New York: John Wiley & Sons).

Brealey, R. A. and S. C. Myers (1996) *Principles of Corporate Finance*, 5th edn (New York: McGraw-Hill).

Bruckner, K, S. Leithner, R. Mclean and C. Taylor (1999) 'What is the market telling you about your strategy?', *The McKinsey Quarterly*, no. 3, pp. 98–109.

Bryan, L. L., T. G. Lyons and J. Rosenthal (1998) 'Corporate strategy in a globalizing world: The market capitalization imperative', *The McKinsey Quarterly*, no. 3, pp. 6–19.

Copeland, T, T. Koller and J. Murrin (1996) *Valuation – Measuring and Managing the Value of Companies*, 2nd edn (New York: John Wiley).

Fama, E. F. (1991) 'Efficient Capital Markets: II', *Journal of Finance*, no. 5 (December), pp. 1575–1620.

Fuller, R. J. (1979) 'Programming the Three-Phase Dividend Discount Model', *Journal of Portfolio Management*, vol. 5 (Summer), pp. 28–32 (New York).

Leibowitz, M. L. (1978) 'Bond Equivalents of Stock Returns', *The Journal of Portfolio Management*, vol. 4, no. 3 (Spring), pp. 25–30.

Leibowitz, M. L., E. H. Sorensen, R. D. Arnott and H. N. Hanson (1989) 'A Total Differential Approach to Equity Duration', *Financial Analysts Journal*, Sept.–Oct.

Leibowitz, M. L. and S. Kugelman (1993) 'Resolving the Equity Duration Paradox', *Financial Analysts Journal*, Jan.–Feb., pp. 51–64.

Leibowitz, M. L. (1986) 'A Total Portfolio Duration: A New Perspective on Asset Allocation', *Financial Analysts Journal*, vol. 42, no. 5 (Sept.–Oct.), pp. 18–29, 77.

Lofthouse, S. (1994) *Equity Investment: How to Select Stocks and Markets* (Chichester: John Wiley).

Markowitz, H. M. (1959) *Portfolio Selection: Efficient Diversification of Investments* (New York: John Wiley).

Roll, R. (1977) 'A Critique of the Asset Pricing Theory's Tests', *Journal of Financial Economics*, 4, pp. 129–76.

Sharpe, W. F. (1963) 'A Simplified Model for Portfolio Analysis', *Management Science*, vol. 9, pp. 277–93.

Statman, M. (1987) 'How Many Stocks Make a Diversified Portfolio?', *Journal of Financial and Quantitative Analysis*, vol. 22, no. 3, pp. 353–63.

Part IV

Portfolio Analysis and Asset Class Theory

6 Portfolio Concepts and Asset Relationships

Portfolio theory and the CAPM

In the theoretical role of portfolio construction, a portfolio's risk is measured in the form of portfolio standard deviation (or variance). From an estimate of the so-called feasible set the efficient portfolio sub-set would be selected that satisfies the conditions of mean-variance rationality, namely:

They dominate by offering the highest expected return at all portfolio standard deviation points; or

They dominate by offering the lowest portfolio standard deviation at all expected return points.

A collection of portfolios is illustrated as an example in Table 6.1. Within this universe, consider the two portfolios B and D. Each offers a standard deviation of returns of 6 per cent and there is an expected return of 15 per cent and 18 per cent respectively. In this instance, an MPT risk-averse investor would select portfolio D, which offers an expected return of 18 per cent. This is illustrated in Figure 6.1. The investor is now left with four choices from the previous five. In this simplified example, the remaining four portfolios would form the efficient portfolio sub-set from the five original portfolios.

Table 6.1 *Example of a feasible portfolio set*

Feasible portfolios	Risk (s.d.)	Expected return
A	5%	13%
B	6%	15%
C	7%	20%
D	6%	18%
E	8%	21%

Figure 6.1   *Example of investor risk preferences under the portfolio characteristics of the CAPM (portfolio D being preferred to that of portfolio B)*

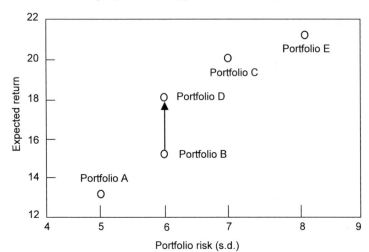

Now suppose that this investor has undertaken the necessary analysis for all combinations of all elements within all the asset classes available and has reduced the number of portfolios to the efficient portfolio sub-set (a simpler ranking device is discussed in Elton, Gruber and Padberg, 1978). This efficient portfolio sub-set would form the higher bound of the plot of standard deviation against expected return and is called an *efficient frontier*. In this approach, the asset allocation is determined as a product of the efficient frontier rather than being determined directly.

The next decision involves which portfolio should be chosen from those lying on the efficient frontier. This can be illustrated as the indifference curve tangency point on the efficient frontier so that each investor holds an efficient portfolio that maximises their utility. Under a common mean-variance rule of behaviour, every investor will generate the same efficient frontier but can still choose to have exposure to different risky portfolios. The CAPM overcomes this by accepting the assumption of borrowing or lending at the risk-free rate (known as the separation theorem: see Tobin, 1958, pp. 65–86). The effect is that every investor will be exposed to the same risky portfolio. This common risky portfolio is formed as the point of tangency to the efficient frontier from a linear equation of equilibrium known as the Capital Market Line (CML). In the language of the CAPM, this common risky portfolio is usually referred to as the *market portfolio*. Portfolios lying on this straight line will be CAPM efficient: that is, they form the set of efficient weighted portfolios.

Figure 6.2   *The CML (as a linear combination of the market portfolio and the risk-free asset)*

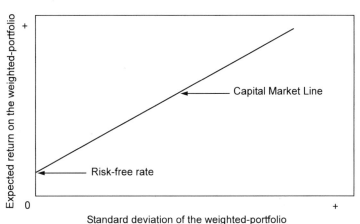

How is the risky portfolio allocated in a chosen portfolio? Consider a weighted portfolio with non-zero weight, w, in the market portfolio and one minus this weight $(1 - w)$ in the risk-free asset. This means the CML will be linear (see Figure 6.2), and since the risk-free asset has a known return that is invariable:

Weighted-portfolio expected return =
(Expected return on the market portfolio) $\times w + (1 - w)$(risk-free rate)

But the expected return on the market portfolio can be represented as the risk-free rate plus the market risk premium so that:

Weighted-portfolio expected return =
Risk-free rate + Market risk premium $\times w$

Further, since the risk-free asset is assumed to have a return that is invariable, it does not add to the risk of the weighted portfolio. Therefore, the standard deviation of the weighted portfolio will be proportional to the standard deviation of the market portfolio according to its weight in the market portfolio.

We can now draw conclusions about the theoretical implications for portfolio construction and individual securities under the CAPM assumptions. Every investor bases conclusions on the same efficient set. With the assumption of lending or borrowing at the risk-free rate, every investor will be exposed to the same risky portfolio formed as the CML point of tangency to the efficient frontier (called the market portfolio), the combination of risk-free asset and market portfolio being varied such that it maximises each individual's utility. This will be reflected in the market capitalisation weights of the constituents in the market portfolio.

The CAPM is an intuitive theory, but there remain antithetical considerations. The CAPM argues that systematic risk forms the measure of individual security risk for a holder of an efficiently diversified portfolio. This is reasonable in so far as a market in equilibrium should not aim to reward risk reduction that has already been reflected in prices, but the model does assume that investors allocate their security holdings in ways that reduce unsystematic risk. In practice, equity markets might also exhibit sector effects (see, for example, Berry, Burmeister and McElroy, 1988 for an empirical analysis of different sector risks taken from arbitrage pricing theory). The CML is determined on the assumption of zero transaction expenses, but in practice expenses will be incurred. These provide an impediment to efficient portfolio diversification. Further, the separation theorem is a useful notion that leads to a determinate solution for the market portfolio. However, a common borrowing and lending rate is unrealistic. A higher borrowing rate needs to be seen in the context of lowering the expected return from every weighted-portfolio comprising borrowing. In practice, therefore, investors are subject to divergent borrowing and lending rates. The set of efficient weighted portfolios will no longer form a continuously linear line across all ranges of risks and the CML will not offer a unique tangency point to the efficient frontier as the equilibrium solution to the market portfolio (although a zero-beta version helps to correct for this). Empirically, support for the single factor CAPM has been mixed (see, for example, the reviews in Lofthouse, 1994).

Given the above, why is the single factor CAPM approach so often referred to by fund managers and analysts? There are a number of reasons because many useful practical concepts have emanated from the model, but more generally it offers a framework for understanding or generalising certain market movements and a conceptual basis for understanding certain strategies. For example, the CAPM beta correlates security expected return with that of the expected return on the market portfolio. However, if the market portfolio is simply viewed as the equity market, some specialised investors aim to neutralise broader market effects. In the context of the CAPM, they aim to maintain a portfolio they believe has a positive alpha (rather than a negative alpha). To help improve the analogy, a desire to neutralise systematic risk means they would also consider the extent of net cash used and (because of potential sector effects) the sector bias in the holdings.

Yield gap relationships

Although the main asset classes tend to be cash, traditional bonds, index-linked gilt-edged stocks, equities and property, let us briefly consider one model of the relationship between an equity index and a traditional gilt-edged market proxy.

Since both bonds and equities can be viewed as discounted cash flow type arrangements, it is not surprising that some researchers have attempted to compare the two models. The notion is centred on the premise that the risk-adjusted capitalisation rate from an appropriate equity market index should be equal to an appropriate bond market yield proxy. In market equilibrium, this leads to the mainstream definition of the (reverse) yield gap:

Dividend growth rate − Equity risk premium

= Bond yield − Prospective dividend yield

The reassessment of UK equities during the 1960s led to an equity market yield lower than that on long-term traditional gilt-edged stock. Therefore, there is no real reason why the risk characteristics of equities versus bonds ought to be equal, and that difference is reflected in an equity risk premium (empirically, this may also reflect differences in the respective markets: for example, relative liquidity). Consider the reasoning by Brealey and Vila (1998) for the period between the beginning of the 1990s and the summer of 1998. Over that period, they observed that the gap between equity yields and gilt yields narrowed. Thus they reason 'that if the risk premium and expected nominal dividend growth have remained constant, then the fall in nominal interest rates was more than sufficient to explain the rise in equity prices in the UK during this eight year period'.

To see the equities in relation to inflation, the (reverse) yield gap is sometimes reformulated by simply deducting the expected inflation rate from both sides still relying in part on the simple assumptions underlying the basic dividend discount model. This can be stated as:

Real dividend growth rate − Equity risk premium

= Real bond yield − Prospective dividend yield

Empirical evidence by Wadhwani (1992: copyright 1992 by Goldman Sachs) supports the view that one reason why equity prices in the 1980s did well, even though the real interest rate was high (for example, relative to the 1970s), was that inflation actually fell. He draws inferences from econometric evidence that support the hypothesis that the equity market was linked to the nominal rate of interest (rather than the real rate of interest). He thus suggests that an improved valuation framework could be better modelled if the real bond yield were substituted for the nominal bond yield in the real (reverse) yield gap model (which would also lead to a different empirical measure for the risk premium). However, Wadhwani (1992) also recognised the possibility that investors might modify their behaviour beyond his econometric evidence period to link dividend yields with the real bond yield. During the four-year period ending in the summer of 1998, Brealey and Vila (1998) observed that the gap between index-linked gilt yields and dividend yields was roughly constant. Thus they reasoned that it was not necessary to call upon a fall in the risk premium or an increase in the expected real rate of dividend growth to explain the fall in equity yields (or rise in prices). They deduced that a fall in real interest rates (based on index-linked gilts) could explain almost the entire fall in yields over that four-year period. Although this is not evidence of a market shift of emphasis from the nominal bond yield to the real bond yield over that period, it does indicate that the real bond yield can also be a useful explanatory variable.

Some active fund managers focus more on the return at the end of their holding period, but few would presumably feel comfortable if that return fluctuated widely in the meantime. Therefore, in looking at assets, a CAPM framework might be useful and this requires three considerations:

- returns;
- standard deviations;
- correlation coefficients.

Statistically, a managed portfolio's beta (we use the same term as that in a CAPM context for want of an alternative) can be recast as the correlation coefficient with the benchmark portfolio multiplied by the ratio of its standard deviation and the standard deviation of the benchmark portfolio. Therefore, the relationship between risk as measured by beta reflects both correlation and relative volatility (that is, relative portfolio standard deviation). The significance of volatility has historically varied according to the asset (see Anderson and Breedon, 1996), but the (reverse) yield gap model emphasises correlated assumptions. This might nòt be so unreasonable in a beta context if volatility were transferred between asset classes, although such a generalisation would fail to consider the magnitude of any transfer and its impact on correlation. Empirically, Anderson and Breedon (1996) investigated the link between UK asset price (return) volatility (standard deviation) using weekly and monthly data on the FT 30 Index (excluding a dividend adjustment), a series of ten-year gilts (where daily data was used, prices excluded accrued interest) and (three-month) Treasury bill markets. Over the

periods 1946 to 1995 and 1972 to 1995, they found that the volatility in the FT 30 share index was transferred to the bond (ten-year) and (three-month) Treasury bill markets. They found no indication from their study that volatility was transferred to the equity market and recognised the possibility of distortion from unsystematic effects in a sample of just 30 stocks, but it does appear that equity volatility has over the study period danced to its own tune.

In considered disequilibrium the (reverse) yield gap relationship is usually related to a mean reversion hypothesis. Further, the equity risk-premium is time variant and as an expected measure cannot be observed *ex ante* while equity earnings and dividends have not been linked in a linear fashion over all past time frames. Perhaps it is for reasons such as these that many fund managers have focused on a less eloquent formulation known as the yield ratio. The dividend yield ratio, in its simple form, takes the ratio of the yield from a sufficiently long bond market proxy and divides it by the dividend yield from an equity market proxy (see Figure 6.3). However, because a dividend yield ratio lacks theoretical rigour, its usefulness will need to be based on practical reasoning (see, for example, the operational discussion in Thomas, Jeffreys and Clare, 1992). Alternatively, the earnings yield might be substituted for the dividend yield in the yield gap (called an earnings yield gap), or in the yield ratio (called an earnings yield ratio) which aims to reflect the relation to earnings.

Figure 6.3   *UK dividend yield ratio*

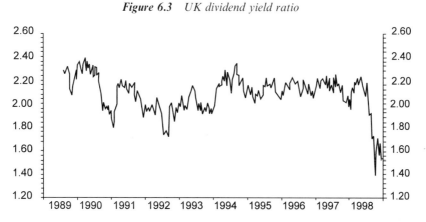

Source: Primark Datastream, reproduced with permission.

Asset allocation and regional allocation

Asset allocation is associated with decisions about the proportion of funds to be invested in different asset classes. The importance of asset allocation to the overall investment decision can be illustrated and put into context by:

Total Fund Return = Asset Allocation Return + Stock Selection Return

In practice, this additive relationship is a somewhat simplified representation because of the exclusion of correlated relations between the two sources of returns. Nevertheless, it highlights that performance is, among other things, a function of both the quality of the asset allocation decision and the stock selection therein.

In considering the asset allocation decision, fund managers generally tend to emphasise two time frames, strategic and tactical. The strategic asset allocation objectives are associated with long-term asset weights within a portfolio. They may be related to benchmark weights or portfolio optimisers, or may be based on a view of what the average fund manager is doing elsewhere. In cases where liabilities need to be met, this essentially will help to dictate the strategic asset allocation bias. The tactical asset allocation objectives are associated with short-term assessments of asset classes. These occur because of relative differences to the long-term forecast outlook for asset classes. The approach may be related to top-down considerations that aim to time the efficient allocation at various stages of a cycle. Alternative approaches include (reverse) yield gap relationships, options ratio analysis or technical analysis. A stock-picking approach to each asset would make allocations across different assets according to individual security analysis. The method by which the weights in a portfolio are controlled also varies. For example, one asset allocation approach does not rebalance the assets on a regular basis, employing more of a passive buy-and-hold strategy. Other examples include maintaining a given weight in a single asset or calculating probabilities of relative performance and relating these to a statistical approach to the decision on the asset weights.

In an international context, regional allocation within assets will usually form an integral part of the overall investment decision. For many UK based global pension funds, the proportion of UK domestic bonds is, at the time of writing, somewhat less than their holding of international equities. In this sense, international diversification and the related strategic and tactical regional decisions will have become a more focused aspect than domestic asset allocation decisions.

To see the relative importance of regional allocation, consider global equity markets over the last fifteen years or so to 1999. The patterns of market behaviour will reflect many considerations, but in large part would be linked to the economic and corporate background. Between 1984 and 1989, the Japanese market increased by more than a factor of three and then fell precipitously without as yet (at the time of writing) returning to its previous high. Asian (excluding Japanese) equity markets showed a similar rising trend during 1984 to 1989 but, after an initial precipitous fall in line with that of the Japanese pattern of equity market prices, subsequently rose culminating in 1997 and then falling precipitously before rising again during the period 1998 to 1999. Latin American equity markets entered a three-year 'bull' market in early 1995 and then fell precipitously in 1997 before rising again during the period 1998 to 1999. The equity markets of the USA, UK and continental Europe have all been, with the exception of an occasional slip, in an upward trend since 1984.

The regional tactical and strategic approach used in a domestic investment context is sometimes modified to apply in an overseas context. The latter aspect might not be so unreasonable from a top-down perspective since at the macro-economic level, similar variables might be relevant although the degree of sensitivity to each variable will tend to vary across different country equity markets. Other approaches may include technical analysis, growth or (deep) value investing, an aggregate bottom-up approach, simply stock picking, indexing or anticipating the international weights of the average peer group benchmark.

With a CAPM mean-variance optimisation framework, the number of estimates required in an asset allocation context usually declines relative to portfolio construction at the individual constituent stock level. Although this means that these estimates can be better controlled, it does not remove the desirability of having a benchmark. This is because it might result in more than one mean-variance mix of assets with equivalent statistical optimisations (see Michaud, 1989). In terms of a benchmark (either with optimisation or other approaches), one consideration in the context of international equities resolves around the benchmark choice with two of the more popular based on market capitalisation or (sometimes) gross domestic product.

References and further reading

Adams, A., D. Bloomfield, P. Booth and P. England (1993) *Investment Mathematics and Statistics* (London: Graham & Trotman (Kluwer Academic Publishers Group)).

Anderson, N. and F. Breedon (1996) *UK Asset Price Volatility Over the Last 50 Years*, Bank of England, Working Paper Series No. 51 (June) (London: Bank of England).

Berry, M.A., E. Burmeister and M.B. McElroy (1988) 'Sorting Out Risks Using Known APT Factors', *Financial Analysts Journal*, March–April, pp. 29–42.

Brealey, R. and A. Vila (1998) 'Equity Prices and Financial Stability', *Financial Stability Review*, Bank of England, issue 5 (Autumn), pp. 10–18.

Elton, E. J., M. J. Gruber and M. W. Padberg (1978) 'Optimal Portfolios From Simple Ranking Devices', *Journal of Portfolio Management*, vol. 4, no. 3 (Spring), pp. 15–19.

Lofthouse, S. (1994) *Equity Investment: How to Select Stocks and Markets* (Chichester: John Wiley).

Markowitz, H. M. (1959) *Portfolio Selection: Efficient Diversification of Investments* (New York: John Wiley).

Michaud, R. O. (1989) 'The Markowitz Optimization Enigma: Is "Optimized" Optimal?', *Financial Analysts Journal*, Jan.–Feb., pp. 31–42.

Thomas, S., R. Jeffreys and A. Clare (1992) 'Redeeming Features', *Professional Investor*, April, pp. 16–20 (London: The Institute of Investment Management and Research).

Tobin, J. (1958) 'Liquidity Preference as Behaviour Towards Risk', *Review of Economic Studies*, vol. 26, pp. 65–86.

Wadhwani, S. (1992), 'Do Global Stock Prices Need to Fall by 40%?', *Goldman Sachs International Ltd.*, 27 March (London: Goldman Sachs International Ltd).

Part V

Equity-Related Options

7 Real Options, Warrants and Convertibles

Introduction

Innovation in financial markets seems virtually endless. Derivatives form one area that has led to a wide array of new innovations as the mathematical and statistical methods from other scientific disciplines have been applied. However, the basic premise remains the backbone to understanding the more complex variations and structures.

The exchange traded option contracts offered by the London International Financial Futures and Options Exchange include a range of underlying assets such as selected UK listed shares, UK equity indices, short-term interest rates, government bond futures and a number of commodities. While exchange traded derivative products broadly tend to be standardised contracts, a parallel market exists for over-the-counter contracts that tend to take more specialised forms. We restrict our discussion to options where the underlying asset (or simply underlying) is equity (ordinary share) with a separate section on real options.

Theoretical arbitrage-free option value boundaries

An equity option is an unusual asset. It is written on an existing underlying equity and allowing for the cost of the option, results in a profit or loss for the holder contingent on a number of considerations, including the price performance of that underlying equity. The holder (or buyer) of an option has contracted via consideration (the *option premium* or *option money*) with a writer (or seller) in order to receive the rights conferred under the option contract. A call option contract entitles the holder to buy (call) the underlying equity, but without obligation. A put option contract entitles the holder to put (sell) the underlying equity, but without obligation. These rights would be available to a pre-specified date (the *expiration date*, *exercise date* or *maturity date*) under a (normally) pre-specified price (the *strike price* or *exercise price*). For traded options, the holder can resell the option to another agreeable counter party. The holder can also exercise the contract throughout the option's life (an American option) or on some specified dates during the option's life (a Bermuda or semi-American option) or immediately prior to maturity (a European option). We deal only with European and American options below.

Let us define:

K	=	constant exercise price (per underlying share);
T	=	term (in years) to expiration of the option;
r	=	force (continuously compound rate) of interest;
Ke^{-rT}	=	present value of the exercise price, per underlying share;
C	=	call option money;
P	=	put option money; and
S	=	the price of the underlying share.

The arbitrage-free option bounds for a non-income generating underlying share are:

American call option:	lower bound (intrinsic value)	$C \geq \mathrm{Max}[0, S - K]$
	upper bound	$C \leq S$
European call option:	lower bound	$C \geq \mathrm{Max}[0, S - Ke^{-rT}]$
	upper bound	$C \leq S$
American put option:	lower bound (intrinsic value)	$P \geq \mathrm{Max}[0, K - S]$
	upper bound	$P \leq K$
European put option:	lower bound	$P \geq \mathrm{Max}[0, Ke^{-rT} - S]$
	upper bound	$P \leq K$

where Max[...] refers to the greatest (maximum) value of the two values separated by a comma in the brackets.

Throughout, we assume these bounds hold (for a summary of a number of empirical studies, see, for example, Gemmill, 1993, Ch. 15). Clearly, these bounds will reflect the effect from movements in the underlying share price. This is illustrated in Figure 7.1 for a European call option. We deal only with call option related notions in this chapter.

The intrinsic value of an American option indicates the realised value if exercised immediately. It therefore forms a theoretical lower bounded condition. Conveniently, therefore, the option money can be viewed as comprising two components: the intrinsic value plus the time value. To see this more clearly, it is useful to compare the intrinsic value bound of an American call option and the theoretical lower arbitrage-free bound for an otherwise identical European call option on the same underlying (non-income generating) share. In this instance, the difference between the two options under consideration is early exercise conferred as a right on the American option

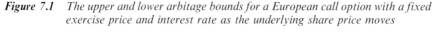

Figure 7.1 *The upper and lower arbitage bounds for a European call option with a fixed exercise price and interest rate as the underlying share price moves*

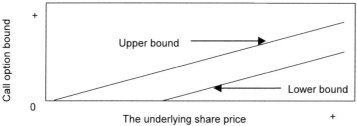

but not on the European option. If the holder intends to retain the underlying share beyond the expiration date, early exercise can be shown to be sub-optimal to the strategy of retaining the option. If early disposal of the underlying is intended then, since the theoretical lower bound of the latter is greater than or equal to the intrinsic value bound of the former, that is, $S_0 - Ke^{-rT} \geq S_0 - K$, early exercise will still not be optimal (as long as the option has time value). The option can be sold in the market. Alternatively, if the American call option is trading below its intrinsic value, arbitrage possibilities become available.

Introduction to option valuation models

To help establish the relationship between an option and its underlying share, quantitative techniques are applied under assumptions to model the sought-after relationships. In the original model, the underlying share return was specified as a random variable under an objective probability distribution. Two approaches then resulted when attempting to evaluate the option: the 'a priori' method, which pre-specifies the value of the parameter inputs, and the 'empirical' method which aims to draw inferences under parameter inputs determined from market information.

To see how the 'a priori' approach can work, two theoretical considerations are often made; first, that equity markets have already incorporated the implications of all known information in prices; second, new information is instantly incorporated in share prices. Share prices or returns are then modelled and the relation to an option measured in a probability sense. One of the simpler probability based option pricing models is that originated by Black and Scholes (1973), which has subsequently been advanced by other authors.

There are a number of mathematical derivations of the Black and Scholes (1973) model relationship (see for example, Hull, 1993, and Adams *et al.*, 1993). Thus, it is not our intention to discuss the mathematics and we need not get involved with the intricacies of the formula detail (an example is reproduced later). However, let us touch briefly on a few aspects as background to the other sections in this chapter.

The Black and Scholes (1973) model makes a number of assumptions when evaluating a European call option. It assumes that volatility and the riskless rate of interest are measured as continuous rates and are fixed throughout the life of the option, and also that there are no transaction costs with the underlying traded continuously without price jumps. The exercise price is assumed fixed. It also assumes that the underlying share price makes no payments of any kind and follows a log-normal distribution over the option's life, and so on.

The underlying share price, exercise price, and the term of the option to maturity are all given or can be observed. The interest rate is usually determined as a proxy in financial markets, so the most subjective input becomes volatility. To help generate more objective insights, model option relationships were used to derive the implied volatility factored in a given option from its market price. The implied volatility measure might be thought to be maturity dependent, but not exercise price dependent. However, it appears that implied volatility can be related to exercise price (see the discussion and references in Gemmill, 1993, Ch. 7). Nevertheless, the perspective of the holder is also important. For example, a short-dated option might be held to maturity. In such cases, the pay-off will be a function of the underlying share price performance to expiration rather than a function of the future implied volatility standing in the market.

One of the versatile European option pricing models is that of the binomial model (see Cox, Ross and Rubinstein, 1979). The model assumes the underlying share price follows a multiplicative binomial distribution, the underlying pays no income and there are no transaction expenses with constancy of volatility, interest rate and exercise price. The binomial methodology takes the term to maturity of an equity option and assumes the share price will move in either of two ways over each discrete time interval. Each discrete time interval is fixed, as is the proportionate up and down share price moves that are determined by the model (see, for example, Jarrow and Rudd, 1983, Ch. 7). The binomial model option value will equate to that of Black–Scholes (1973) in the limit as the number of discrete periods in the options life tends to infinity (see, for example, Adams *et al.*, 1993, Ch. 20).

To see the (delta) hedge ratio, consider the following simple example of a binomial share price diagram (see Figure 7.2) (with the corresponding value of the call options at the various nodes in parentheses). Now consider the theoretical hedge ratio given by the model. For example, starting at the node

Figure 7.2   *Example of a simple binominal share price diagram*

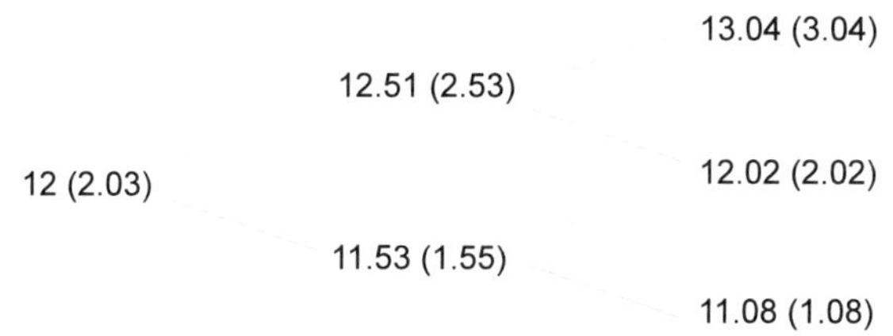

```
                                                    13.04 (3.04)
                             12.51 (2.53)

            12 (2.03)                               12.02 (2.02)

                             11.53 (1.55)
                                                    11.08 (1.08)
```

Note: All figures rounded

given by a share price of 12.51, the model assumes a share price at the end of a further discrete time period as either:

(a) 13.04 so that the hedge ratio at $S = 12.51$, $^{S}\Delta_{12.51}$ requires:

$$^{S}\Delta_{12.51}12.51 - 2.53 - \text{present value of } (^{S}\Delta_{12.51}13.04 - 3.04) = 0;$$

(b) 12.02 so that the hedge ratio at an underlying share price of 12.51, $^{S}\Delta_{12.51}$ requires:

$$^{S}\Delta_{12.51}12.51 - 2.53 - \text{present value of } (^{S}\Delta_{12.51}12.02 - 2.02) = 0$$

with the present value of the expressions in parentheses calculated over the discrete period at the riskless rate of interest. In both cases, $^{S}\Delta_{12.51}$ ought to be equal. Therefore, solving the simultaneous equations for this example gives the binomial hedge ratio as $^{S}\Delta_{12.51} = 1$ (rounded).

Clearly, the hedging strategy introduced in Chapter 1 is highly abstract. This does not change with a simplified adaptation that removes the need to vary the amount of the riskless asset. One effect of such a simple delta hedging approach is that the financial burden changes so that although it remains theoretically riskless, it is no longer theoretically perfect. In part, this is because the delta hedge (and thus 'the share equivalence' of the option) position will remain in place only for an infinitesimally short space of time, reflecting the continuously dynamic nature of the theoretical hedging strategy.

Although each hedging strategy forms a purely theoretical argument that is based on assumptions that are mostly unrealistic, the Black–Scholes (1973) theory has been suited to offering insights in more practical situations. One of the less obvious arises in the strategic value of options when seen in terms of certain real business situations. Viewed as an analogy to financial options, this forms the subject matter of the next section.

Real options

As noted in Chapter 4, company management can be proactive to its environment. This is more obviously so when required to make long-term capital investment decisions. It is in this context that this section is included here. It relies heavily on the extracts taken from an article written by Leslie and Michaels (1997, 'The real power of real options'), who aim to provide a framework on the strategic value of real options. We reproduce only a selection of extracts from their article below.

One of the characteristics of an American call option written on an underlying equity is that it provides a holder with an option to buy, wait or sell in the light of new information. Excluding transaction expenses then, at maturity, for example, if the intrinsic value is positive, the holder will find that the optimal choice is to exercise; if the intrinsic value is negative, purchasing the underlying in the market forms a more optimal route to owning the underlying. One can well envisage financial options situations as analogues to certain business situations encountered in real life. As Leslie and Michaels (1997) note:

'Advocates of real options suggest that the thinking behind financial options may be extended to opportunities in real markets that offer, for a fixed cost, the right to realize future payoffs in return for further fixed (that is, independent of the asset value) investments, but without imposing any obligation to invest. Seen in these terms, the parallel between owning a North Sea oil licence and owning an option on Merck stock becomes clear. By paying a fixed licence fee to the government, the oil company buys a real option: the right to realize payoffs at any time over the next five years by making further fixed investments (independent of the future value of the oil block), but with no obligation to develop the block.'

With these kinds of real business situations, there is an obvious analogy with financial options that Leslie and Michaels (1997) define as *reactive flexibility*. Less obviously, the authors reason that real options – that is, options in certain real business situations – can also offer *proactive flexibility*: the flexibility to take actions in ways that enhance the value of a previously acquired option. This helps to differentiate real options from financial options:

'Some flexibilities are obviously common to financial and real options. In each case, an option holder can decide *whether* to make the investment and realize the payoff, and if so, *when* to invest – important, since the payoff will be optimal at a particular moment. These are essentially *reactive* flexibilities: flexibilities an option holder exploits to respond to environmental conditions and maximize his or her payoff.

When we talk about the reactive flexibilities of a real option, however, we are ultimately talking only about its advantages as a valuation tool. The further, typically larger, payoff comes from the *proactive flexibility to increase the value of an option, once acquired.* This opportunity arises from the fact that, whereas a financial option is acquired and exercised in a deep and transparent market, real business situations usually feature a limited number of players interacting with one another, each of which can influence the real-option levers and hence the option value.

A manager in a pharmaceutical company, for example, has the flexibility to influence a real-option lever such as the present value of a project's cash inflows (stock price) by increasing the resources put into marketing. He or she might be able to increase the option's duration (time to expiry) by securing a product patent or renegotiating a licensing agreement. These actions would, of course, also affect the value of the options held by other players.

The advantage of proactive flexibility is that management can use their skills to improve an option's value before they exercise it, effectively making it worth more than the price paid to acquire or create it' (Leslie and Michaels, 1997).

Leslie and Michaels (1997) consider a dividend modified Black–Scholes (1973) form (see Merton, 1973):

'The price of a financial option is typically estimated by the application of the Black–Scholes formula:*

$$Se^{-\delta t}\{N(d_1)\} - Xe^{-rt} \times \{N(d_2)\}$$
$$\text{where } d_1 = \{In(S/X) + (r - \delta + \sigma^2/2)t\}/t^{1/2}$$
$$d_2 = d_1 - \sigma t^{1/2}$$

and where S = stock price, X = exercise price, δ = dividends, r = risk-free rate, σ = uncertainty, t = time to expiry, and $N(d)$ = cumulative normal distribution function.' (Leslie and Michaels' note * reads: 'The original Black–Scholes formula calculates the theoretical option value – the present value of the expected option payoff – under the assumption of no dividend payments, taxes, or transaction costs. The above formula, as modified by Robert Merton, incorporates dividends (δ): it reduces the value of the share to the option holder by the present value of the forgone dividend, and reduces the cost of holding a share by the dividend stream that would be received.') [The notation used in the above formula and in the note have been modified from that found in the electronic version of the article by Leslie and Michaels, 1997.]

To relate this to real option situations, it is possible to align the definition in the parameter inputs under the simple financial option valuation theory with an analogy that Leslie and Michaels (1997) reason can be extended to real options. For example, stock price has a real option analogy as the present value of the cash inflows from the underlying asset. Exercise price has the analogy as the present value of all the expected fixed costs taken over the life of the underlying investment opportunity. In a financial option, volatility (sometimes generally described as uncertainty) corresponds to the expected standard deviation on the underlying stock returns. An analogy in a real option framework is the standard deviation of the growth rate of the value of future cash inflows associated with the underlying asset. The Merton (1973) form of option valuation theory also caters for dividends. Since many stocks pay dividends, a real option analogy would be the value lost during the life of the option. The authors explain that dividends

> 'are sums paid regularly to stockholders. In real-market terms, dividend expense is represented by the value that drains away over the duration of the option. This could be the costs incurred to preserve the option (by staving off competition or keeping the opportunity alive), or the cashflows lost to competitors that go ahead and invest in an opportunity, depriving later entrants of cashflows.' (Leslie and Michaels, 1997)

They further reason that reducing this can be seen in terms of the value lost in waiting to exercise. For an American call option written on a dividend paying underlying share, situations might arise that make it optimal to exercise the option immediately before the underlying stock goes ex-div, taking into account the opportunity cost of not exercising. In the context of real options, Leslie and Michaels (1997) explain:

> 'In a real business situation, the cost of waiting could be high if an early entrant were to seize the initiative.* When first-mover advantages are significant, the dividends are correspondingly high, thus reducing the option value of waiting. The value lost to competitors can be reduced by discouraging them from exercising their options: by locking up key customers or lobbying for regulatory constraints, for example.' (Leslie and Michaels' note * reads: 'We use an already committed player to make the parallel with financial options perfect, because the dividend is paid to a current (rather than a potential) shareholder. In real options, one could extend this logic to include potential entrants without doing serious damage to the analogy.')

Time to expiration is the period to maturity of the option and in real options 'will depend on the extent of technology (product life cycle), competitive advantage (the intensity of competition) and contracts (patents, leases and licenses)' (Leslie and Michaels, 1997). Although a change in the risk-free interest rate, *ceteris paribus*, has an effect on model-based option values, it is not an issue in proactive flexibility because the effect of any strategic business initiative would presumably not influence it.

Before going on, consider the following example by Leslie and Michaels (1997) under the dividend modified Black–Scholes (1973) option valuation theory:

'Consider again the oil company valuing its licence blocks. This is a classic example of a real option, in which paying the licence fee (acquiring the option) gives the owner the right to invest (at the exercise price) after uncertainty over the value of the developed reserves (stock price) is resolved.

In a similar case, another oil company has the opportunity to acquire a five-year licence on a block. When developed, the block is expected to yield 50 million barrels of oil. The current price of a barrel of oil from this field is, say, $10, and the present value of the development cost is $600 million. Thus the NPV of the opportunity is simply:

$500 million – $600 million = –$100 million

Faced with this valuation, the company would obviously pass up the opportunity.

But what would option valuation make of the same case? To begin with, such a valuation would recognize the importance of uncertainty, which the NPV analysis effectively assumes away. There are two major sources of uncertainty affecting the value of the block: the quantity and the price of the oil. One can make a reasonable estimate of the quantity of the oil by analyzing historical exploration data in geologically similar areas. Similarly, historical data on the variability of oil prices is readily available. Assume for the sake of argument that these two sources of uncertainty jointly result in a 30 percent standard deviation (s) around the growth rate of the value of operating cash inflows. Holding the option also obliges one to incur the annual fixed costs of keeping the reserve active – let us say, $15 million. This represents a dividend-like payout of 3 percent (ie, 15/500) of the value of the asset. We already know that the duration of the option, *t*, is five years and the risk-free rate, *r*, is 5 percent, leading us to estimate option value at

$$\text{ROV} = (500e^{-0.03 \times 5}) \times \{(0.58)\} - (600e^{-0.05 \times 5}) \times \{(0.32)\}$$
$$= \$251 \text{ million} - \$151 \text{ million} = +\$100 \text{ million.*'}$$

(Leslie and Michaels' note * reads: 'This valuation is simplistic in that it makes a restrictive set of assumptions (such as log-normal distribution of asset value and constancy of dividend, uncertainty, and interest rates) that are imposed by the analytical approach.')

So where does that difference in value come from? The authors provide one explanation in terms of flexibility value as follows:

'Ultimately, then, the option valuation recognizes the value of learning. This is important, because strategic decisions are rarely one-time events, particularly in investment-intensive industrial sectors. NPV, which does not properly recognize the value of learning more before a full commitment is made, is for that reason often inadequate. In fact, its inadequacy can be stated in the precise terms of the real-options model. Of the six variables in that model, NPV analysis recognizes only two: the present value of expected cashflows and the present value of fixed costs (Exhibit 2 [Figure 7.3]). The greater comprehensiveness of option valuation can therefore be summed up in this way: it captures NPV plus flexibility value – effectively, the expected value of the change in NPV over the option's life.

Figure 7.3 *Comparison of valuation methodologies*

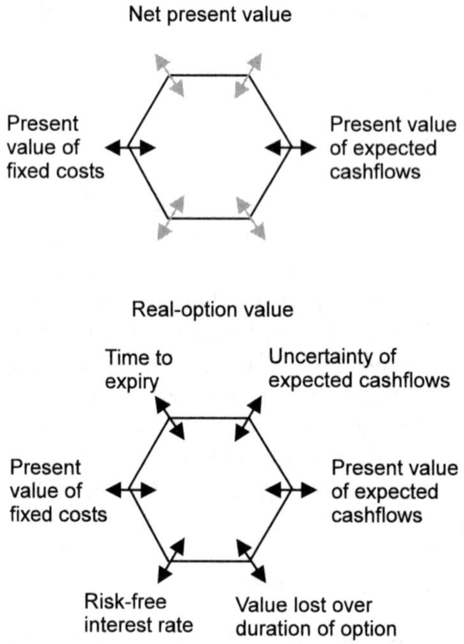

Net present value

Present value of fixed costs — Present value of expected cashflows

Real-option value

Time to expiry   Uncertainty of expected cashflows

Present value of fixed costs — Present value of expected cashflows

Risk-free interest rate   Value lost over duration of option

Essentially, NPV can mislead whenever there is flexibility, especially flexibility to respond to uncertainty over the rate of cashflow growth, because it incorporates only two key levers of value creation. It assumes, that is, that the present values of both cash inflows and cash outflows are static. Practitioners who are aware of NPV's shortcomings tend to rely on techniques such as scenario analysis to capture the fact that these values must necessarily be *ranges* and not single numbers. Using high, low, or medium scenarios helps to bound the uncertainty, but it does not help to incorporate into the valuation the variance across the different scenarios. Scenario thinking recognizes that uncertainty exists, but does not capture the flexibility value inherent in a situation, and hence offers little managerial guidance. In contrast, real options provide a comprehensive valuation model for any strategic situation, however uncertain.' (Leslie and Michaels, 1997)

In financial options, a sensitivity analysis is used to determine the significance of changes in different parameter inputs on option value under the *ceteris paribus* condition. Because each situation will be different, the relative sensitivities will vary according to each case. In the context of real options, Leslie and Michaels (1997) draw on the above hypothetical real-option situation as an example:

'Which levers should a company pull? Which levers can it pull? The first question is one of economic priority, and can be determined by a straightforward sensitivity analysis.

Take, once again, the example of the licence blocks, which real-option valuation judged to be worth $100 million, and NPV analysis *minus* $100 million. As Exhibit 4 [Figure 7.4] shows, sensitivity analysis of the six levers quickly identifies potential economic priorities. The exhibit shows the effect on option value of a 10 percent increase in each lever. We see immediately that, as with the valuation of any option, changes in the lease's duration, the risk-free interest rate, and the annual cost of the lease (or value lost over the duration of the option) have less effect than changes in the present value of expected cash inflows and cash outflows and the level of uncertainty. A 10 percent improvement in each of these levers adds about 26 percent, 16 percent, and 11 percent respectively to the value of the option.

So it appears to be better to focus on getting revenue up than on getting costs down – a key insight in option value management. There are, of course, external constraints such as competition or market regulation. But even if it should turn out that the more powerful levers are less easily influenced, the analysis reveals that improving duration and "dividend" (ie, annual costs) by 10 percent can together yield a significant return.

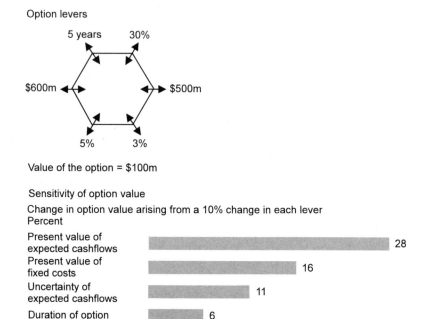

Figure 7.4   Pulling the real option levers

The question of which levers can be pulled is simply one of the internal and external constraints on the operations of the company. These might be technical, or have to do with marketing, negotiating, or contractor management issues. They would also concern investment-specific factors such as the delay between investment and payoff and the indivisibility of investments (that is, constraints on incremental investment).' (Leslie and Michaels, 1997)

Essentially, the strategic initiatives that a company can take in certain real business situations to enhance the value of a previously acquired real option (proactive flexibility) adds differentiation to a financial option. This is also significant, but usually more complex, in certain business situations where exercising a real option not only generates cash flows, but also a further option (see Copeland and Keenan, 1998).

Equity call warrants

An equity warrant is similar to an equity call option. It involves the call option holder with a purchase right on the underlying share and the issuer with a contingent obligation in such event. The purchase of the underlying at exercise is usually allowed in the form of cash and this is what we shall assume. Participants in the warrant market sometimes attempt to take advantage of warrant gearing or leverage sensitivity to an expected move in its underlying although the motive force to owning or writing a warrant does vary.

The exercise of a warrant will usually mean a new issue of underlying shares. This means, unlike a call option issued on existing shares in the market, that new shares will be issued on the exercise of an uncovered warrant. In the case of a covered warrant, the writer (usually a financial institution) will undertake to cover the exercise rights of the warrant. This cover can take various guises. On the one hand, the issuer may dedicate an existing holding of shares to the contract. On the other hand, the issuer might simply agree to cover the liability if and when the warrant is exercised from the existing pool of shares trading in the market. Most warrants do not have a terminal value if they are not exercised, but might have provision to vary the exercise terms in the event of a share split or the offer of new shares in lieu of dividends. Some warrants may have additional features such as an initial waiting period before the warrant can be exercised. Most warrants are either European (exercisable only at maturity) or American (exercisable up to maturity) with a fixed exercise price; they have no additional features. It is with these warrants that we will be concerned in this book. For simplicity, we shall also assume a covered warrant on a non-dividend paying underlying ordinary share (unless otherwise noted) without a waiting period.

The analysis of equity warrants encompasses a myriad of tools and techniques. Each would have its own advantages which would help to highlight particular measures of sensitivity to the underlying. We briefly look at a number of the simpler ones below.

The choice of either purchasing the warrant or the underlying share means that it is possible to differentiate between the two. To see this, one approach for European warrants relates the possible returns from the underlying share price and the warrant over the life of the warrant (or to the optimal exercise date if earlier for American warrants). If i is the annual compound growth rate in the underlying share price, S, and warrant, the *capital fulcrum equation* is:

$$S \times (1 + i)^T - K = \text{Warrant price} \times (1 + i)^T / \text{Warrant ratio}$$

where warrant ratio = the number of underlying shares one warrant entitles the holder to purchase; K is the exercise price; and T is the time to warrant

Figure 7.5   *An example of the break-even warrant price(s) for various share price growth rates assuming $S = K$*

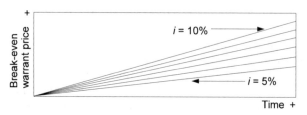

expiration. This can be rearranged to solve for the *capital fulcrum point* (the solution to i in the capital fulcrum equation). As the fulcrum point changes so will the required percentage change in the share price to equate to the percentage change in the warrant price. Or equivalently, the required percentage change in the warrant to equate to the percentage change in the share price will change. Clearly, the future share price at the fulcrum point growth rate rises as the fulcrum point rises. The fulcrum approach, although somewhat crude, highlights the importance of the underlying share price on the ultimate performance of a warrant. Consider Figure 7.5. This shows a specific example of the break-even warrant price(s) for $S = K$ at various share price growth rates. As the rate of growth in the share price (i) rises, the break-even warrant price is seen to increase. For example, the break-even warrant price at $i = 10\%$ is seen to be greater than the break-even price at $i = 5\%$.

As a valuation tool, however, the fulcrum methodology is rather simple. It simply assumes the standing value of the warrant. Also, consider an analogy from the Black–Scholes (1973) model. The capital fulcrum point can then be seen in terms of the risk-neutral valuation methodology, such that the capital fulcrum approach does not factor the volatility on different underlying shares. Further, it does not take account of interest rates or any dividends on the underlying. Theoretical arbitrage arguments suggest that a warrant (per underlying share) ought to cost less than the underlying share so that some investors derive investment implications by equating the capitalised interest savings from owning the warrant to the capitalised dividends forgone from not owning the underlying shares directly. However, such a DCF approach does not allow for the effects of warrant gearing although it would highlight the fact that a lower dividend lowers the forgone income to the warrant.

Now consider an American warrant. One variation of what is known as the *parity value* can be viewed as the pay-off from a warrant if it was exercised immediately. Thus:

Parity value = Warrant ratio × Market price per underlying share

The amount by which a warrant is in-the-money or out-of-the-money can then be given as:

Warrant (intrinsic value) = Parity value − Warrant ratio × K

Similarly, one variation of what is known as warrant *premium* can be viewed as the percentage amount over the parity value that would have to be incurred (excluding transaction expenses) in buying a warrant ratio number of shares through simultaneous purchase and immediate exercise of a warrant (an American warrant). In notation:

Warrant premium (%) = $[(W/K + 1)/(S/K) − 1] \times 100$

where: W = warrant price/warrant ratio (that is, the warrant value per one underlying share).

To help make more meaningful relatives between warrants of different maturities, the premium is often calculated as a compound annual rate. For example, consider the previous example again and, assuming the market price of the underlying share is 20, the premium is:

Warrant premium (%) = $[(11/12 + 1)/(20/12) − 1] \times 100$

= 15% over six months (or 32.25% as a compounded annual rate)

Warrant gearing defines the money needed to purchase one unit of the underlying directly relative to that of the price of the warrant. Thus:

Gearing = Parity value/Warrant price

= S/W

Consider a generalised example of gearing as a warrant increases by one unit amount when the price of the underlying is fixed given $W < S$. This is illustrated in Figure 7.6. If the upper arbitrage bound, $W \leq S$, is satisfied, then warrant gearing will be greater than or equal to one. For example, consider a warrant priced at 5 on an underlying share priced at 10 and warrant ratio of 5. Gearing is:

Gearing = $10 \times 5/5$

= 10

The expected percentage sensitivity of a warrant to small movements in its underlying is known as *leverage* or *elasticity* and this is a function of a

Figure 7.6   *Illustration of warrant gearing as warrant money (W) rises in steps by 1 unit assuming an unchanged underlying share price (S) for W ≤ S*

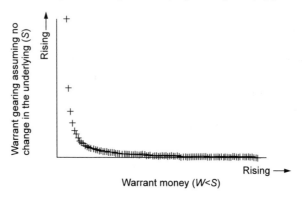

warrant's delta and gearing. However, break-even analysis investigates the required change in a warrant to a small change in its underlying share price for the two to break even. Consider the premium per cent for an American warrant again. For example, if the corresponding percentage rise in $W/K + 1$ is less than 1 per cent for an instantaneous 1 per cent rise in S (even if W rises proportionately more), the premium per cent will fall. If the corresponding percentage fall in $W/K + 1$ is less than 1 per cent for an instantaneous 1 per cent fall in S (even if W falls proportionately more), the premium per cent will rise. This is illustrated in Figure 7.7. To see this, consider the break-even percentage change in W that makes these scenarios borderline:

Break-even percentage change in $W = K/W + 1$

For example, if $K = 100$ and $W = 10$, then the break-even percentage change in W is 11 per cent. That is, if W increases by more than 11%, then $W/K + 1$ will increase by more than 1 per cent, meaning the premium per cent will rise for an instantaneous 1 per cent rise in S and vice versa.

A call option valuation model's generated delta defines the proportionate change in a call option's premium for a small change in the underlying share price, *ceteris paribus*. However, from the break-even percentage change in W, the break-even delta can be determined under the no-arbitrage condition given warrant gearing. A break-even delta defines the proportion by which a warrant is required to change to match a given small change in the underlying share price. If a warrant satisfies the arbitrage free bounds, then the break-even delta will be equal to or greater than one.

Although break-even delta is derived independently of the other normal model considerations (though mathematically the same analysis could have been generated from the Black–Scholes (1973) model when this generates the

Figure 7.7 *Illustration of the relationship between an American warrant's premium per cent for a 1% change in S as W/K + 1 varies*

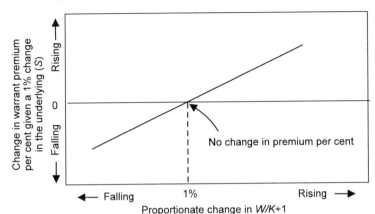

same warrant value), it is sensitive to the standing value of the warrant. Thus it can suffer by assuming the standing value of the warrant because a warrant can still take a range of values before being unbounded by its arbitrage-free conditions. This is illustrated in Figure 7.8, which relates premium per cent and break-even delta for an American warrant under its theoretical arbitrage free bounds as the ratio of the share price to the constant exercise price varies.

To assess the standing value of the warrant, an option valuation approach is sometimes applied. Looking at a warrant as a long-dated call option, the following are considerations:

• current price of the underlying share price;
• exercise price;
• volatility of the underlying share;
• remaining time to expiration;
• interest rates;
• dividends on the underlying share.

Of course, warrants have specific differences to exchange traded call options that might be thought to require additional factor considerations. Warrants are typically written with longer lives, and when issued on new shares the claims on the firm by existing shareholders might become diluted. However, if the share price has correctly factored dilution, then similar factors adjusted to the situation can still be seen to be relevant in most situations (this is discussed in Gemmill, 1993, Ch. 12).

Figure 7.8   *Example of the theoretical arbitrage-free bounded valuation diagram for an American warrant as the underlying moves linearly*

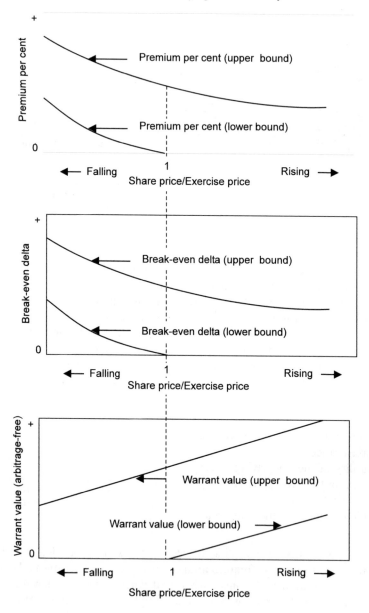

Equity convertibles

An equity convertible security is a hybrid corporate security with characteristics associated with both a fixed-income security and equity. Equity convertibles emerged as a balanced solution to a desire for equity but with the preferential advantages of many fixed-income type of instruments. If the underlying equity does well, the convertible holder will potentially benefit by exercising the right to conversion. If the underlying equity performs badly, the convertible is a relatively safe banking proposition compared to the underlying equity because of the extra covenant of a preferential income stream (although the extent of fixed-income type rights can vary between different convertible issues).

Unlike a call option that can be exercised, an equity convertible security (hereafter referred to simply as a convertible) is converted into (or surrendered for) the underlying equity (some convertibles have permitted satisfaction of conversion rights for cash, in many respects a bond plus warrant). Often, the conversion option applies over a continuous time period (the conversion period), but can be restricted to specified dates, and sometimes there is an initial waiting period before conversion is permitted. A convertible will normally have a finite life, although perpetual variations have been issued. While it is traditional for conversion to result in the issue of new shares, some convertibles are issued by a third party (not necessarily a financial organisation) for which the underlying equity has been covered from the existing pool of shares in the market.

A convertible might allow conversion once a year. Other issues can be exercised on more than one date, and some have call features whereby the issuer can call (or redeem) the convertible benefits early. This feature might be linked to the underlying share price having appreciated above a certain level or may occur under other circumstances. The call price is usually fixed at issue, but convertibles have been issued with provision for this to vary by periodic amounts over the life of the convertible. If the issuer exercises the call option, the holder is usually given the opportunity to convert rather than accept the call price being offered. Rational investors would choose the most profitable alternative and issuers sometimes exercise their call rights at a time when the call price is relatively unattractive, and thus entice conversion. If a convertible is called, it may not always be the case that the holder is entitled to accrued coupon on the bond (although they might then be entitled to the next dividend payment on the underlying equity if converted). Some convertible issues incorporate a put option where the holder has the right to sell the convertible benefits back to the issuer at a put price (or prices). Although this makes a convertible issue more attractive to investors, it also means that the issuer can be called upon to fund an exercised put at a time when refinancing is more costly.

Convertible bonds generally have a plethora of different terms and conditions and features. These would include such areas as any protection afforded in the event of a scrip or rights issue, accrued coupon entitlement on conversion, early repayment options, the circumstances where voting rights may apply and the exact nature of the bond protection and any protective clauses. Market conventions also vary as to the preponderance and emphasis on different valuation criteria. In this book, we have restricted our discussion to fixed-income convertible securities issued in the domestic (pound) sterling markets without early repayment options.

Historically, when a sterling convertible was first issued, the issue price was often set such that its price sensitivity was closest to its underlying equity. Because of the hybrid nature of convertibles, over subsequent periods the relative sensitivity might vary between the underlying equity or the bond element. It also means that situations might arise where the sensitivity of a convertible to its constituent elements is not clear. Thus a number of approaches have evolved, with each offering particular insights.

Some investors separate a convertible package into its income-generating element (the fixed-income element of a convertible) and its option value. Therefore, one way of looking at a convertible is as a bond plus option:

Convertible bond value =

Non-convertible fixed-income security plus call option

The option element might be estimated using option valuation models. However, apart from considering the potentially longer life of a convertible and the potential impact of issuing new shares on existing shares, conversion requires the 'exercise' of the call option and the surrender of the fixed-income benefits. Viewed in this way, a convertible is seen to differ from a warrant or call option, since the 'exercise price' is based on the convertible rather than being fixed. Simpler valuation models make the assumption that the stock return is the only stochastic (random) variable and so allow for the risk characteristics of the bond element using a yield premium. More advanced arrangements not only explicitly model the credit risk itself, but also make a stochastic interest rate assumption.

A convertible's parity value can be defined in various ways. We shall define it as the conversion ratio (the number of the underlying equity one convertible bond entitles the holder to receive on conversion) multiplied by the market share price (a definition we continue with although parity value has also been defined such that it also allows for the yield difference to the convertible). The discounted cash flow relationship attempts to measure the income receipts from owning the convertible relative to the dividends forgone from not owning the underlying shares directly. These cash flows can be capitalised so that the difference between the income received from the convertible relative to the income from the parity value can be estimated. This difference in present value of income (DPVI) would usually be calculated over the period of whichever is the earlier, the maturity date or the date at which the income from its parity value exceeds the income from the convertible. The more positive the DPVI, the greater the discounted cash flow advantage of the convertible relative to its parity value.

Some investors view a convertible price as the sum of its parity value and its premium (or discount):

Convertible price =

Parity value + Value of convertible premium (or discount)

For example, a convertible trading at 100 on a coupon pay-date (excluding that coupon) with a conversion ratio of 10 on an underlying share trading at 8 will have a conversion premium of:

$$\text{Value of premium} = 100 - (10 \times 8)$$
$$= 20$$

or

$$\text{Premium } (\%) = 20\%$$

Imagine a convertible standing at a premium as (i) the sum of its parity value and its discounted cash flow advantage and (ii) the sum of its parity value and its premium amount. Equating these two perspectives reduces to equating the DPVI against the conversion premium amount and indicates why the DCF advantage is often associated with a return of the conversion premium. Rather than determine a cash advantage, this approach is often modified to determine an implied dividend growth rate that would equate the resulting dividends from the parity to the convertible premium amount. One of the simpler variations is the pay-back period that aims to establish the time point at which the amount over the parity value will be compensated for by any extra income advantage of the convertible. Whilst the DCF approach tends to adhere to a more consistent logic by considering both the timing of the cash flows and the time value of money, a number of 'rules-of-thumb' approaches have evolved with the pay-back period (see Fabozzi, 1997, Ch. 42).

Theoretical arguments are sometimes used to illustrate a relationship between premium per cent and changes in the underlying parity value. Imagine a hypothetical situation of a convertible whose non-convertible bond element (sometimes referred to as the straight bond value of a convertible) is constant. If a convertible's parity value rises, then, for example, a convertible price that rises by the same amount will have a conversion premium per cent that falls. If a convertible's straight bond value remains constant but the parity value falls, then, for example, a convertible price that falls by the same amount will have a conversion premium per cent that rises. In practice, the bond element will not remain constant and the default risk of the bond element might also vary. For example, if the default risk were to increase, the sensitivity between parity value and a convertible's straight bond value might also increase, so distorting the convertible premium path for changes in just parity value. While some investors view convertibles more as possible bond substitutes, the potential dominance of the parity value over the straight bond value on convertible performance derogates this argument because it highlights the potential significance of the underlying share price on convertible valuation. The significance of this will tend to increase as the convertible price sensitivity to its underlying parity value increases.

Consider another specific example where the last day for conversion also falls on the maturity date of a convertible (this is a simplification for ease of illustration since convertibles do not usually permit conversion on the actual maturity date). Should this convertible still have a premium? To prevent arbitrage opportunities in a market with no transaction costs and excluding the impact of issuing additional equity, the convertible should be worth whichever is the greater, its parity value or its redemption value. For example, suppose that at maturity the choice for a convertible owner is to receive a parity value of 80 on conversion or a redemption value of 100. A rational holder would choose the redemption amount.

Consider the discounted cash flow advantage again. Suppose it can be extended beyond in time such that with continued dividend growth it becomes a disadvantage (that is, negative). Assuming a simple constant change in the discounted cash flow advantage (disadvantage), an example is illustrated in Figure 7.9. If beyond the date that the discounted cash flow advantage becomes zero (the break-even point), the convertible value (viewed as the

Figure 7.9 *Example of the theoretical relationship between a given parity value and DCF advantage/disadvantage*

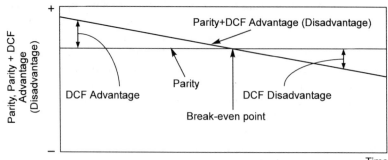

parity value plus the discounted cash flow disadvantage) relative to the parity value will decline with the passage of time, as the discounted cash flow disadvantage increasingly becomes more negative. In such instances, the discounted cash flow advantage approach would have potential implications for the optimal timing for conversion. However, this consideration might not initially be the dominant factor for some investors when, for example, the sustainability of dividend on the underlying parity is in doubt.

In practice, a convertible can at times trade at a discount to its theoretical straight bond or parity value (see Morton, 1995, pp. 26–7). This might reflect, for example, market inefficiencies or the relative performance expectations of the convertible relative to its straight bond or parity value. Although this is potentially distortive, at the two extremes of convertible behaviour – when the parity value is significantly above or below a convertible's straight bond value – sensitivities would generally tend to be more obvious. Between these two extremes, it becomes more difficult to make sensitivity generalisations (except perhaps in the form of a well-specified probabilistic model or statistical sensitivity analysis).

Other derivatives contracts

Option contracts include those written on interest rates, currencies, stock indices and options on futures (see, for example, Hull, 1993, and Fabozzi, 1997); futures contracts include those written on short-term interest rates, government bonds, stock indices, agricultural products (commodities) and currencies (see, for example, Hull, 1993, and Adams *et al.*, 1993); for the more esoteric and exotic financial securities see, for example, Galitz (1995).

Closing words

In this book, we have been able to introduce only a few of the models of security analysis and were constrained to touch on only some of the many insights they can offer. We also gave examples of the link between theory and practice and although this is clearly a complex phenomenon, an appropriate analogy can help to offer a wealth of fascinating insight.

References and further reading

Adams, A., D. Bloomfield, P. Booth and P. England (1993) *Investment Mathematics and Statistics* (London: Graham & Trotman (Kluwer Academic Publishers Group)).
Black, F. and M. Scholes (1973) 'The Pricing of Options and Corporate Liabilities', *Journal of Political Economy*, vol. 81, no. 3 (May/June), pp. 637–54.

Copeland, T. E. and P. T. Keenan (1998) 'Making Real Options Real', *The McKinsey Quarterly*, no. 3, pp. 128–41.

Cox, J. C., S. A. Ross and M. Rubinstein (1979) 'Option Pricing: A Simplified Approach', *Journal of Financial Economics*, Vol. 7 (September), pp. 229–63.

Fabozzi, F. J. (editor) (1997) *The Handbook of Fixed Income Securities*, 5th edn (New York: McGraw-Hill).

Galitz, Lawrence (1995), *Financial Engineering, Tools and Techniques to Manage Financial Risk* (London: Financial Times/Pitman Publishing).

Gemmill, G. (1993) *Options Pricing: An International Perspective* (Maidenhead: McGraw-Hill)

Hull, John C. (1993) *Options, Futures, and Other Derivative Securities* (Englewood Cliffs: Prentice-Hall International).

Jarrow, Robert A. and Andrew Rudd (1983) *Option Pricing* (Homewood, Illinois: Richard D. Irwin).

Leslie, K. J. and M. P. Michaels (1997) 'The real power of real options', *The McKinsey Quarterly*, no. 3, pp. 4–22.

Merton, R. C. (1973) 'Theory of Rational Option Pricing', *Bell Journal of Economics and Management Science*, 4 (Spring), pp. 141–83.

Morton, J. (editor) (1995) *Global Guide to Investing* (London: Pitman Publishing).

Taylor, F. (1996) *Mastering Derivatives Markets* (London: Pitman Publishing).

Index

Index